SPELLS FOR BEGINNERS, REVERSAL & PROTECTION MAGICK

SPELLS FOR BEGINNERS, REVERSAL & PROTECTION MAGICK

Published 2023 by Sofia Visconti

LEGAL NOTICE:

DISCLAIMER NOTICE:

SUBSCRIBE TO SOFIA VISCONTI

Greetings!

As a subscriber, you will receive a **Free Gift** + you will be the first to hear about new books, articles and more exclusives **just for you.**

Simply scan the qr code to join.

CONTENTS

CURSE BE GONE

THE BOOK OF SPELLS FOR BEGINNERS

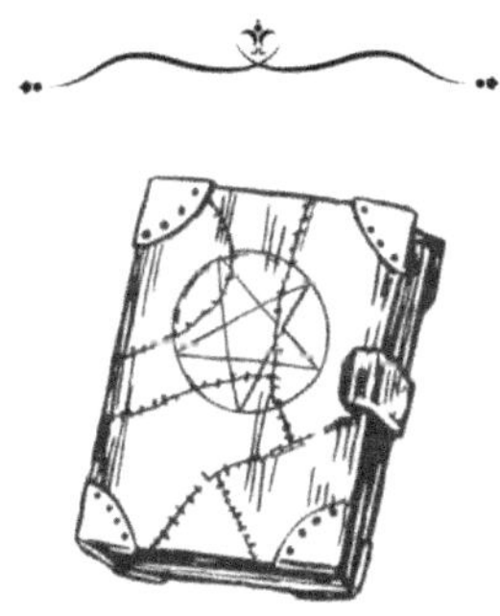

INTRODUCTION

When someone thinks about magic spells, one may be inclined to think of two different things. The first is the wicked witches with boiling cauldrons and flying brooms, cursing those they dislike and causing havoc wherever they go. The second is the wand-wielding (or staff-wielding) wizard who invokes words of power to cast their magic for either good or evil. However, this book isn't about magic spells. It is about magick spells.

Unlike fictional magic, magick does not have the power to turn people into frogs or summon fireballs from thin air. Instead, magick and its craft offers a more subtle approach. Spellcasting using magick offers a way to focus on your life and give you power to achieve your goals. This power is practically invisible compared to the theatrical powers of witches and wizards, but unlike them, this power is real.

Some readers at this point may be skeptical of such claims. Many will claim that magick is just parlor tricks that are on par with illusionists. However, the truth is that magick is a spiritual experience. In order to properly cast spells, the first step is to open yourself up to the possibility that it exists. If you dismiss magick, no spell you cast will work. You need to have faith in yourself and the spell in order to see results. That is the first step you need to realize if you want to cast spells.

Other readers may be asking who is able to tap into magick. The simple answer is anyone. Unlike fictional works, anyone can cast a spell. It doesn't matter what gender or age you are; anyone can cast a spell. That being said, where you are when you cast the spell does matter, both emotionally and physically. Additionally, most spells need more than simple words in order to work. There is a more complex answer to this though, as this book will show the loose nature of magick and its many forms.

This guide exists to help beginners learn about basic spellcasting. However, this book does more than just explain how one can cast spells. It also goes over the history surrounding the exploration of magick and provides a beginning spell to use for practice. This book also goes over common materials used for spellcasting, enabling beginners and just curious users to experiment with creating spells. It also goes over other practices of spellcasting, as this book focuses primarily on a general form of Wicca. That is not to invalidate the other practices. It is simply because Wicca usually describes itself as practicing witchcraft through various means. There are even some Wiccans that adopt practices from other practices with historical roots. This diverse and freeform way of spellcasting is arguably better for a beginner as they can start off where they feel most comfortable. At the same time, if you wish to go for more complicated practices, that is fine as well. This book is merely a guide to the basics and a jumping off point for further research.

Some might be asking what are the benefits of casting spells. The answer depends on what spell you want to cast. Some spells help improve your well-being. Others  enhance your focus and foster better reflection on what you want out of life. A few can help cleanse the body and offer protection from vile things. Alternatively, some spells could be used to invoke pain towards someone you dislike, but it is not advised that you do such spells. Those hurt by magick might seek retribution, which can be dangerous depending on how much damage was dealt. Remember, use magick to better yourself, not to tear others down.

CHAPTER 1
MAGICK

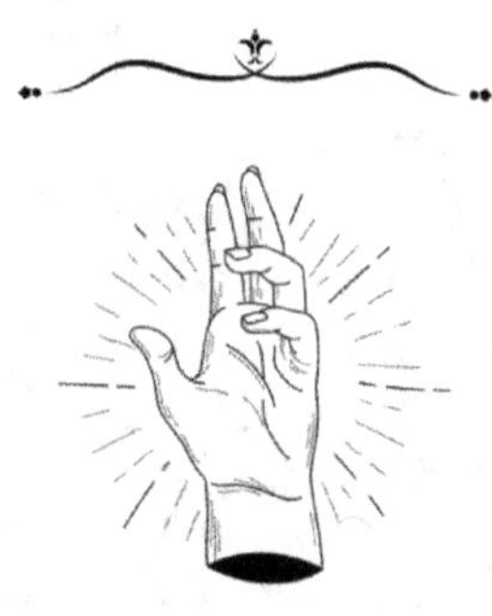

Before we begin planning out our first spell, we first need to understand the nature of magick. Magick comes from the natural elements within our universe, similar to fictional forms of magic. These elements vary from practice to practice, but each source comes from a fundamental part of our universe. Nature has magick found in the plants that grow around the world. Stars and planets have magick within them, making predictions about a person's future. Stones and crystals can be attuned to better harness magic. There is magick in our thoughts and emotions. Even numbers have some magick about them. There is magick everywhere. It just takes time and a bit of effort to harness it.

Once harnessed, magick can be used to influence the world. Not change, not shift, not alter. Influence. Magick cannot work by itself to make the world a better place or make you achieve your goals. It is simply a helping hand, a way to help accomplish your desires. Just like a person helping you out, though, you need to put in effort as well. Some may point to this fact as a reason to believe that magick has no power, which is an incorrect conclusion. It is a subtle force, but a force that will get the job done if you put in just as much effort.

Some might ask where these ideas come from. In truth, these ideas were formed in separate times by different people. Some fuse these ideas together, seeking to connect magick from all sources. Others view these ideas as separate, putting importance on some while discarding others. There is no unified answer on which sources are more powerful or more reliable. However, even if one doubts the validity of a source, one cannot deny there is history behind them. A history that can often be cruel.

Witchcraft

The origins of witchcraft and witches is a complicated one. That is because many cultures around the world have separate ideas of what constitutes a witch, making it hard to pinpoint which witches are the oldest. For Europeans, some may point to the Bible's Book of Samuel, where King Saul sought a witch to summon a prophet to aid him (History.com Editors, 2017). Others claim that honor belongs to Circe from Homer's *Odyssey* who turned men into animals (Purkiss, n.d.). However, across the Atlantic, the Navajo have their own type of witch. The skinwalker was a witch that could disguise themselves as an animal. And Africa has a history of cannibalistic witches who feast on human blood (Lewis & Russell, n.d.). As one can guess, historical witches were often seen as evil people who sought only personal gain.

As time passed, the idea of witches changed, especially for European witches. With the rise of Christianity, the concept of witches strayed away from the biblical verses that portray witches as communers with the dead. Instead, the Christian faith began to view witches as agents of Satan. This was especially emphasized in the book *Malleus Maleficarum* written by Heinrich Kramer. The book asserted that witches were solely evil in nature and that their spells were aided by the Devil. His book helped inspire witch hunts for centuries.

While many reading this may know of the Salem Witch Trials, they weren't the first instance of a witch hunt. Those trials in 1962 were just one of many that happened after the publication of the *Malleus Maleficarum*. In fact, trials like these predated the book by about six decades, with the earliest noticeable witch trials happening in the early 15th century in Valais, a region in modern-day Switzerland. Starting in 1428, these trials took the lives of 367 supposed witches. In stark contrast to the Salem Witch Trials and other witch trials, the majority of the accused were men.

A thing to note is that many of these witch trials were conducted over a span of years, some lasting entire decades before finally dying down. Additionally, while some had a sudden stop in accusations, others slowly died out with small periods of new cases coming in. The motives behind the trials also change from period to period, with some being religious while others were motivated by selfish desires. However, after the Valais Witch Trials, the *Malleus Maleficarum* became part of the tool kit for new witch hunts across Europe.

A few of these witch hunts include:

- The Trier Witch Trials of 1581, taking place in the Holy Roman Empire, were a notable series of trials as they are often considered to be one of the largest witch hunts in history.

- The North Berwick Witch Trials in 1590s Scotland.
- The Fulda Witch Trials of 1603, where over 200 Germans died after being accused of witchcraft.
- The Pendle Witch Trials of 1612, where the 12 accused were tried in Lancashire, England.
- The Bamberg Witch Trials of 1627, another German witch hunt with a confirmed death toll of 884 victims (Connolly, 2016).
- The Torsåker Witch Trials started around 1668 in Sweden, but reached a climax in 1675. On one day in that year, 71 accused were beheaded and burned.

While European witch hunts have now become their metaphorical counterpart, other cultures still practice the horrible act. People are still being blamed for the misfortunes of others, even if the person in question doesn't believe in magick. Depending on where you are, you could still be accused of being a witch and face mob justice. While the lack of witch trials in the United States and in Europe may seem like a benefit, the solution to that issue was the creation of a new one. In return for no longer being persecuted, fewer people would believe in the power of witches.

Though science is not a replacement for spirituality, many people believe that it is. The truth is, science can't answer everything without being highly immoral or impractical. At the same time though, science that has been researched for years cannot be replaced by spirituality. The rejection of years of scientific research only results in one making a fool of themselves, and it can further damage the reputation of all spiritual beliefs. Science and the belief in the supernatural may clash from time to time, but both can coexist if practiced in certain ways. Even if people may disagree with that point, they can't deny that witchcraft is still being practiced today.

Not all of modern witchcraft is an extension of earlier practices. This is partially due to the fact that what was considered to be "witchcraft" in older eras were actually practiced by people amongst different faiths. Most often these older systems would be named something else, like "Heka" or "Wu," with the majority of them being attached to a religion. Nowadays, witchcraft is most often associated with a singular group: the Wiccans. While some Wiccan covens still practice traditional rituals, the Wiccans as a whole wish to remove the bad connotations often associated with witches.

While the practices and organization of Wiccan groups can be traced to earlier sources, the name "Wicca" was first created by Gerald Brosseau Gardner. Born in 1884, Gardner was raised in Lancashire, England. His first exposure to occultism started when he moved to Malaya (now known as Peninsular Malaysia) as a civil servant for the English. During his time there, he was exposed to rituals and beliefs conducted by the region's Indigenous peoples. Showing keen interest in these subjects, Gardner began to research into them further, even submitting his work to the *Royal Asiatic Society* journal on his findings in regards to early civilizations of Malaysia (*Gardner, Gerald Brousseau,* n.d.).

Gardner returned to England in the 1930s,

where he encountered a coven in Highcliffe, England. This opened Gardner's eyes to the European side of mysticism. This sudden interest was dangerous at the time since English law still outlawed the concept of witchcraft, even if many doubted the harm witchcraft could produce. Despite the threat of legal repercussion, Gardner wrote his first book while in England, calling it *High Magic's Aid*. To evade persecution, he published the book under the pen name "Scire" (*Gardner, Gerald, Brousseau*, n.d.). This danger would later be removed following the end of World War II. In the 1950s, England repealed their laws against witchcraft, allowing Gardner to openly publish one of his most famous works, that being *Witchcraft Today* in 1954 (Wigington, 2019a).

Witchcraft Today introduced the word "wica" to a larger audience, a word Gardener had encountered while interacting with the coven at Highcliffe (History.com Editors, 2018b). The book is composed of Gardener's various theories, experiences, and rituals conducted while being with the Highcliffe coven. With this book, Gardener created his own coven, whose practices influence much of Wicca today. By the time of his death in 1964, Gardener's version of Wicca, known as Gardnerian Wicca, had acquired a decent amount of awareness.

It should be said that this was merely the start for the modern Wiccans. Time had passed since then, and there are many different variations of the practice. Even during Gardener's time, Wiccans were changing, as the second "c" wasn't used until the 1960s (History.com Editors, 2018b). One point that never is truly agreed upon is the definition of a witch. What defines a witch can vary from person to person, some using the term politically while others use it spiritually. Witchcraft is a very loose term that could apply to many things, which works well as the history and current practices can vary greatly between covens.

Due to this loose application, the concept of witches has expanded enough that people have classified witches into different groups. While witches aren't exclusively a single type, the use of such terminology can help one define themselves when talking to other spellcasters. The easiest witch terminology to understand comes when discussing the difference between a "Coven Witch" and a "Solitary Witch." Coven witches are witches that form a group and work together to cast spells and practice their craft. Solitary witches are witches that practice their craft alone, though it doesn't exclude them from talking to other witches about it. These two categories are so broad that literally every witch fits into one of these two categories, though nothing is stopping them from being both.

Despite the rise of Wicca, traditional witches still exist who practice the craft with methods rooted in tradition and history. Because traditional witches encompass a vast array of beliefs  and practices, it is more likely that a traditional witch would reference the exact belief system they use in their practice instead of simply calling themselves a traditionalist.

Meanwhile, cosmic witches fuse witchcraft with astrology, a topic that will be discussed later. While certain traditional witches may use parts of astrology, cosmic witches base their magick solely on astral bodies. Due to the nature of astrology, some may argue that cosmic witches were one of the most accepted types of witch in a historical context, though that will be looked into more as we explore astrology later on.

Ceremonial witches take the craft very seriously. While all witches have to conduct rituals, ceremonial witches do so in a more intense fashion, doing spells that are very time consuming to conduct properly. It is advised that a beginner should be wary when joining a ceremonial coven due to the rigid nature of the spells.

Unlike the rigid nature of ceremonial witches spells, eclectic witches take a more personal approach to spells. Eclectic witches are witches that basically fuse the components of different witchcrafts together to form a personal one, allowing for a witch to feel more connected with their craft. This book does lean towards that type of witchcraft as well, as this book takes bits and pieces from several different crafts.

Green witches are witches that mostly use the elements of nature to do their spells. Witches who practice this usually try to get close to nature when doing their spells, such as going outside or growing the very plants they use in their rituals. Green witches try their best to connect with the Earth and the life that sprouts from it.

Elemental witches are similar, but instead they focus on gaining their magick through the use of four or five elements. These elements are water, fire, earth, air, and sometimes spirit, but not always. Their spells try to harness these elements either with direct material from those elements or through a representation of them.

A witch that could be seen as a fusion between

green witches and a water-focused elemental witch is called a sea witch. Sea witches share the quality of the green witches in the sense that they too get their spellcrafting materials from nature, though it is more often associated with aquatic or beachside life. Like elemental witches, the sea witch focuses on the element of water and bases a good portion of their craft around it. Sea witches don't neatly fit in either, however, as they exclude the forestry of the green witches and the other elements of the elemental witches.

There are also some types of witches that could be considered odd to some people. Despite the claims that witchcraft must be connected to some deity or spiritual force, secular witches exist to disagree. While not exclusively atheistic, secular witches believe that their practice is not tied to any divine or unholy beings. Their practice is separate from any form of religion, though that doesn't stop the individual witch from believing in one. They simply separate their craft from their faith.

Another type of witch that might be confusing for some is a kitchen witch. While it may seem odd, kitchen witches perform rituals in their home kitchens, usually during the creation of food. They are often known to infuse their dishes with magick, using herbs in a similar way as a green witch. Kitchen witches may also expand their craft to the entire household, though their major place of casting is within the kitchen. Their spells most focus on the food they prepare, with the aim being to enhance both the dish itself and those who consume it.

As one can see, the history of witches is a complex but often tragic one, though today is a much different story. While not everywhere is safe, more people in the modern-day are accepting of the concept of witches, with certain media portraying witches as helpful and kind people. There are still portrayals of wicked spellcasters, but that has hardly stopped the rise, spread, and diversification of witchcraft. There is still some distrust from certain communities about the practice, but it is rarely dangerous to be a witch in the modern-day.

Astrology

A lot of witchcraft focuses on natural elements as the basis of their beliefs. These can include anything from plants to animals, rocks to mountains, moon to stars. Astrology focuses only on the last pair along with other astral bodies such as other planets. The most popular aspect of astrology is the zodiac, though few know the history surrounding it.

Like witchcraft, the zodiac is incredibly old, with the first one being made by the Babylonians back before the B.C. turned into the A.D. The zodiac divides the year into 12 separate parts, each one aligned to a certain constellation. While the constellation is fixed to a certain time of year, astrologists also examine the surrounding region for other astronomical bodies. These bodies include every planet in our solar system, the Sun, and the Moon. Despite the Sun and Moon not being planets, astrologists call all influencing bodies "planets," which can raise some confusion. For the sake of simplicity, "planets" in this section will be referring to the astrologist's definition, not the astronomers.

Each planet is tied to a certain human quality. This quality is shifted depending on the position of a planet in relation to a person's zodiac. The qualities of each planet are as follows:

- The Sun is tied to a person's sense of self-worth, confidence, and ego. It is also tied to masculinity.
- The Moon influences the more instinctive side of a person, such as dealing with emotions and intuition. It is also tied to femininity.
- Mercury is the main influencer of a person's logical and communicative abilities.
- Venus is connected to love and artistic expression, as well as the attractions created by such things.
- Mars is associated with passion, both in the good ways and the bad ways. While Mars is a symbol of courage, it is also used to symbolize conflict and aggressiveness.
- Jupiter is connected to a person's luck, prosperity, and sense of hope.
- Saturn is connected to strength, discipline, and the need to follow the law.
- Uranus is connected to freedom, individuality, and chaos. In other words, Uranus reflects qualities opposed to Saturn.
- Neptune is seen as the planet that

influences one's spirituality and dreams. However, it also represents deception and illusionary thinking.

- Pluto is connected to transformation and the death of the old. It is tied to a person's personal growth.

Each of these planets also rule over one or two zodiac signs. This rulership simply means the planets influence people with those signs more than others. The most important factor though when considering zodiac signs is a person's birth. The zodiac of a person is determined by their date 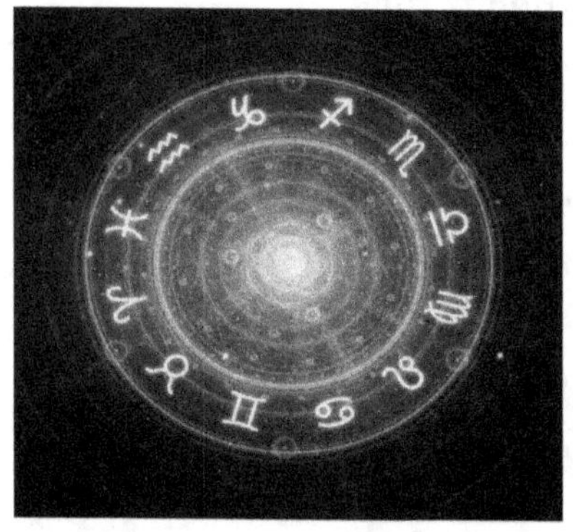 of birth, and the position of the planets in relation to that zodiac may help predict the personality of the person as they grow up. The 12 signs of the zodiac are: Aries, Taurus, Gemini, Cancer, Leo, Virgo, Libra, Scorpius, Sagittarius, Capricorn, Aquarius, and Pisces.

While the Babylonians first created the zodiac, astrology was further developed during the Roman Empire. An astronomer, mathematician, and geographer by the name of Ptolemy was born in 100 A.D. While famous for his geocentric theory of the universe, Ptolemy is also one of the most influential figures when it comes to astrology. In the book *Tetrabiblos*, Ptolemy inscribed the practice and beliefs of western astrology. This book is still one of the most authoritative works and is a must-have for anyone who wishes to study the subject.

While the work of the Babylonians and Ptolemy would dominate astrology for the Western world, in Asia, a different zodiac dominates. The Chinese zodiac works almost identically to the Babylonian zodiac, though there are some differences. While both use constellations, the Babylonian version uses both humanoid and animalistic interpretations of said constellations. Additionally, the names of each sign is Latin for another word. For example, Sagittarius is Latin for "archer" and Scorpio is Latin for "scorpion." The Chinese zodiac uses only animals, both for their naming and their symbols. The animals in this zodiac are: Rooster, Dog, Pig, Rat, Ox, Tiger, Rabbit, Dragon, Snake, Horse, Goat, and Monkey. Additionally, unlike the Babylonian zodiac, which changes over the course of the year, the Chinese zodiac only changes at the end of each Chinese calendar year. The zodiac still has twelve symbols, but it takes twelve years to go through all of them once. Other than those two major differences, the two zodiacs work similarly enough in modern-day, as both can be used to form predictions for daily life.

However, astrology has fallen much since its historical roots. During the Age of Enlightenment, many of the theories surrounding astrology began to be questioned. While astrology did compose of the zodiac and its predictions, the subject also was the source for all astrological knowledge, including planetary alignment and rotational positions. This included Ptolemy's geocentric model, which early astronomers began to pick apart even before the Age of Enlightenment. However, this Age of Reason began to tear down the concepts of mysticism and spirituality to focus more on scientific analysis. While religion was still important to many of the Enlightenment's thinkers, with the consensus saying that all religions should be tolerated, the authority behind astrology began to fade away.

It was only recently that astrology began to regain the attention of the general public. Astrology returned in the 20th century, though in a much smaller format. In the past, the zodiac predictions were typically applied to large populations. Nowadays, the zodiac has been reduced to predicting individual human behavior, with daily horoscopes offering predictions and advice to individuals. These predictions can be very extensive, with some being applied to workplace relations and romantic compatibility. However, those who do practice it are often seen as being ridiculous, claiming that you can't predict things from planetary alignments.

Numerology

While magick consists of a lot of physical items, runes also play an important part when it comes to spellcasting. These symbols carry weight on the spiritual level, and such symbols come in various forms. One set of runes that many might find unorthodox to use for magick is numbers. Numerology uses numbers in order to make predictions in a similar way astrology does with the stars.

The history surrounding numerology is as

complex as witchcraft. Multiple civilizations have employed a form of numerology as a way to diviniate their actions. One of the most popular versions, Pythagorean numerology, came from the observations created by a Greek philosopher by the name Pythagoras. He was renowned for his developments in mathematics, astronomy, and music theory. His study of mathematics led him to develop his numerology method, where a person uses both their name and their date of birth to make predictions about their life. This was done through two different equations.

The first equation requires one to convert the month, day, and year into a singular number. This is done by first converting the month into its numerical equivalent (i.e. January would be one, February would be two). Then each digit has to separate from their whole number (i.e. 1953 would separate into one, nine, five, and three). Then all of the numbers are then added up. This process repeats until the resulting number is either a singular digit or it becomes what is considered a Master Number which are numbers that have significance within a numerology system. For Pythagorean numerology, these are the numbers 11 and 22.

The second technique requires the use of one's full name. In order for this process to begin, the person has to replace each letter with a numerical equivalent. While this may seem difficult already, there is a second layer to this. Instead of simply replacing the letter with its numbered position, Pythagorean numerology limits the letter to a single digit number. In order for this to work, the sequence starts with one for "A", ends with nine for "I", then resets the counter to one for "J." This has to be done with a person's full name. Once that is done however, the process is simple. Add up the single digits together repeatedly until you reach a single number for each part of the name. Then add those digits together until you reach a Master Number or a single digit.

These two equations have different purposes according to Pythagoras. The first equation is used to predict one's path in life, offering insight into one's personality, beliefs, and skills. The second equation is used to help determine what will help a person reach their destiny. The single digits and Master Numbers all have different meanings depending on the equation. These equations were adapted as time went on, as Pythagoroas existed around 600 to 500 B.C. and the original was based on the Greek calendar and alphabet.

However, while the Pythagorean form of numerology is one of the most popular versions, it is not the oldest. The Chaldean version of numerology predates Pythagoras, originating

from a group of people living in Babylonia. For the most part, Pythagorean and Chaldean numerology systems work the same with two key differences. Chaldean numerology only goes up to eight, not nine. Additionally, unlike Pythagorean numerology, the Chaldean system uses a nonconsecutive numbering system. For example, the letter "F" is turned into an eight, not six. The second difference is that the Chaldean system has a third equation associated with it. This equation is done by translating each letter in a person's full name to their numerical equivalent and adding it up. The resulting number is not reduced, as this double digit has its own meaning attached to it, usually pertaining to events that haven't happened yet in one's life.

Another version of numerology was created by early Hebrews. This system of numerology, Kabbalah numerology, is nearly the exact same as

Pythagorean numerology. The only difference is that Kabbalah numerology only cares about a person's name, ignoring the date of birth entirely.

An additional system is Tamil numerology, which was made by a group of people in India who share the same name. This system has the exact same letter to number system as Chaldean numerology, but has two additional equations. While both systems have the name sum equation, Tamil numerology includes a reading for the sum of a person's birth date. These readings come from both the number day itself (i.e. the sixth or the seventh of a month) and the birth date in full.

Numerology, just like witchcraft, has a complex history and multiple systems to consider. While they come from separate sources and have varying readings, most claim to come from a similar source. The source of power does vary a bit, but it is usually associated with vibrations. These vibrations aren't literal vibrations, instead taking more of a mental force, one that exists subtly in everyone's life, even if they don't realize it. Through the vibrations of these numbers, magick is created, and through it we are able to predict or analyze a person's personality, dreams, and challenges they might encounter in the future.

CHAPTER 2
MATERIALS

In modern culture, stories depict spells being sent out through wands or overly large staffs, magical energy sparking and crackling to life in the air around them. Other stories simply have someone wave their hands around in a certain motion to send out energy. Out of the two, the former is much more accurate to one's manipulation of magick, though it is far from the truth when it comes to presentation. Most spells don't use sticks to direct them, and many don't require a person to be in the same room as their target. Instead, what makes those interpretations more accurate is the use of physical objects. While some spells may not require items, the vast majority of them do. Likewise, not every spell shares the same required materials, so knowing what items are required is important.

Due to the nature of magick, mixing random materials together may not be the best idea. One can easily claim that you need candles, crystals, and herbs, but what can't be easily explained is the meaning behind these items. Each one has a symbolic meaning attached to them, making it important that one pays attention to any spell recipe they come across. Using the wrong materials for a spell could cause unpredictable consequences, especially if you replace one material with a material that symbolizes its direct opposite.

Other items you may need for spellcasting include incense, rope, string, and, yes, sticks. The type of paper may also be important, as many say that parchment paper is the best or only way to cast spells. For beginners, a lot of these items can be found online, as there are online stores that sell spellcasting materials. Just be careful with some of the materials.

Candles

Whenever witches are portrayed as vile hexers, candles are not far behind. Most often, candles are shown around a pentagram with a group of spellcasters summoning a demon from whatever underworld that universe has. Despite this negative connotation, candles are important for spellcasting. More importantly, their use goes beyond summoning spirits or, more oftenly shown, demons. However, like everything else in the spellcasting ritual, the type of candle you use is important. This can include anything from their size to their shape, and even to the candle's scent. However, the most obvious difference in a candle's purpose comes from their color.

White Candles

The color white, in terms of color spectrum, reflects all colors in equal amounts. White candles fit a similar role, where they can be used in replacement of another color. However, such a tactic is not suggested if you want a very potent effect. It can do any candle's job, but other candles do specific tasks better. That is not to say that white candles are entirely worthless when compared to other candles, as white candles do specialize in certain spells.

Protection is one such aspect. Just as the color white repels light, white candles reflect negativity and ill omens. In crafting or focusing on spells that are meant to protect yourself or a loved one, white candles are the way to go. Additionally, white candles can heal or cleanse negativity from a space or person if it would be too late to cast a protection spell. Such cleanses can help improve a person's mood and allow their mind to be free of doubts and pessimistic misconceptions.

Black Candles

Because they are considered opposites in many circumstances, one may expect that black candles are harmful in nature. The truth is the exact opposite. Not to say the colors themselves don't act as opposites. Unlike the color white, which reflects all light, the color black absorbs all light. In practice though, black candles are used to absorb negative energy, focusing all that negativity into itself. This inverse method produces the same overall result to a white candle in terms of negativity removal. However, black candles are considered more effective when it comes to protection, as they absorb the problem, not simply repel it.

Red Candles

Red candles have two sides to them. On one side, red candles can be used to invoke inner strength and passion. Spells meant to boost confidence and courage will often employ red candles. On the other side, red candles are associated with something more promiscuous. Red candles are often used in spells to help boost physical performance, and that performance includes the bedroom. Mind you, spells aren't powerful enough to coerce people to go to bed with you (nor should you ever try even if they did), but they can help make the experience more enjoyable.

Orange Candles

While red candles boost confidence in physical activities, orange candles are used to boost emotional drive. Spells employing orange candles are usually meant to increase one's ambition and  good fortune. They can also be used to increase one's energy if they feel drained after a taxing experience, such as a long day after work or after hearing sad news about a celebrity. Many also claim that orange candles can be used to increase one's joy, though that quality could be attributed to their energy rejuvenation property. The lack of energy could feel uncomfortable to some, so a reverse to that condition would in turn improve a person's mood.

Yellow Candles

Just like the other warm colors, yellow candles are meant to boost an aspect of oneself. Specifically, yellow candles are used to increase one's mental capabilities. Spells using these candles can boost focus, intuition, and aid in recalling events, a perfect combination if one is expecting to face a mental test in the future. Other spells using such candles help improve one's creativity, allowing for new ideas to blossom. This creativity is not limited to artistic ventures, as a sales pitch needs as much creativity as a short story. The only difference between them is that a sales pitch is trying to convince people it's true.

Green Candles

Green candles are used in spells aimed at increasing one's bounty. What this "bounty" entails depends on the spell. This can include some traditional prospects, such as fertility or better harvests. Other prospects include financial wealth or increasing one's luck. Green candles can also be used as a way to rejuvenate oneself or help nurture personal growth. If a spell requires something to increase, usually a green candle is involved.

Blue Candles

Blue candles are usually meant for spells that attempt to calm a person. While white candles specialize in countering negative thoughts, blue candles are specialized in countering angry thoughts. Spells using blue candles are often centered around finding inner peace and to center oneself from any thoughts that could result in actions you might later regret. Beyond relieving anger, this inner peace can also grant wisdom, truthful insight, and inspire loyalty between two people. Because of this, spells pertaining to such qualities usually use blue candles.

Purple Candles

Purple candles are most often used for more spiritual spells. These spells can include anything from delving into ancient wisdom, allowing further insight into a certain situation, or in rare cases allowing a person to have visions. These spells are often harder to do as it takes a lot of dedication to pull these off correctly. Alternatively, purple candles are used to increase one's self esteem and decrease stress. Notably, spells meant to counter insomnia regularly use purple candles.

Pink Candles

Pink candles are similar to red candles in the fact that they both deal with love. However, red candles focus on the physical aspects of love. Pink focuses on the emotional side of love, with spells focused on growing a bond between individuals. This bond doesn't have to be romantic, however. Spells using pink candles can range from helping to find new friends to cementing the bond between two partners. These spells aren't mind control, so don't assume that these can make someone madly fall in love with someone else. Spells using pink candles can also be focused on oneself if needed. Pink candles can promote compassion, self-love, and increase one's empathy.

Brown Candles

Brown is a very earthly color, only rivaled by the color green. Because of this, brown candles are usually used in spells concerning nature or stability. When it comes to its nature half, brown candles are more often used in spells concerning animals, usually to establish a bond with them. In terms of stability, brown candles are often used to bring someone back down to earth. While other candles are specialized in finding inner stability, brown candles are often used in spells concerning the environment around them. In some sense, brown candles could be seen as the opposite of purple candles. While purple candles provide spiritual wisdom, brown candles offer earthly advice. If you plan on doing a spell that requires a purple candle, it might be wise to have a brown candle on hand to recenter yourself.

Silver Candles

Silver candles in some Wiccan circles are considered the most divine. This is because silver is said to represent the Goddess, a deity whose nature varies slightly from coven to coven. However, Wiccans that create altars usually have a silver candle on it in order to share their faith. Beyond that, silver candles are used in spells meant to aid someone's intuition and protect them from unwanted chaos. Sometimes gray can be used in place of silver, but there is some debate about whether or not the two shades mean the same thing.

Crystals

Crystals are a bit of a complex issue when it comes to spellcasting. On the one hand, some claim being in the mere presence of the crystals can cause their effects to go off. On the other hand, some claim that you need to do a ritual for it to work. On a random third hand, you have those, including other spellcasters, claiming that crystals don't work at all. In truth, this debate is a complex one, and the nature of each gemstone varies from type to type. Just be wary when purchasing one if you do, as some crystals could be fake.

Crystals and gemstones are often given healing properties, aiding people fight off stress and illness. However, despite the nature of these stones, it needs to be said that you should still go to a doctor if you are sick. Crystals can aid in healing, but when it comes to illness, nothing is stronger than medicine. Think of gemstones as support that helps you on your road to recovery. Medicine is still the car you need to drive down that road.

Another thing about crystals is the fact that there are a lot of them out there. The sheer number of possible choices as well as some differing opinions about certain gemstones makes it hard to make an entire list detailing each and every one. So instead, here are some popular crystals and what they are used for:

- **Agate:** A multicolored stone that is used to help heal old wounds and to help aid in accepting one's own feelings. It is also used to better one's sleep, both in terms of dreams and the amount of energy the person has the following morning.

- **Amber:** In truth, this isn't a crystal, but a fossilized substance that comes from tree sap. However, the transformative nature of this material means that it is often used to turn negative energy into positive energy.
- **Amethyst:** A purple crystalline quartz, amethyst is used primarily to aid in relaxing one's mind from stress or anxiety. It aims at increasing one's focus while keeping them calm.
- **Garnet:** This red gemstone is often associated with blood, but not in the harmful sense. Instead, it is meant to ease a person of any pain that might come from any blood problems they may be experiencing.
- **Jade:** A gemstone once used for a variety of tasks, it is now used to help a body's natural healing process, specifically when it comes to the internal parts of the body.
- **Rose Quartz:** A pink quartz, this gemstone focuses on helping form bonds with other people. Whether it be romantic love or friendship, this gemstone aids in creating relationships with other people.
- **Sapphire:** A gemstone that is typically

blue, sapphires are often associated with wisdom and spiritual knowledge. Having one may aid you in finding the right words to say and wisdom to back those words up.

These are only some examples and not everyone agrees about their usage. You might have to experiment with crystals to see which ones actually have magick properties and which ones are just duds.

Herbs

Like crystals, there are so many herbs that listing them off one by one could and has filled up books. Unlike crystals, however, more practitioners accept the authority of herbs when it comes to their use in rituals. That being said, you shouldn't go out in the wild to collect herbs if you are new to pharmacognosy and botany as you  might pick up dangerous plants by mistake. Additionally, while you can grow your own herbs, you aren't really expected to as a beginner. Do not worry though. Plenty of websites sell herbs at decent rates. All you have to do is know which herbs you are looking to use and a way to keep your herbs organized.

Other books are dedicated to the planting, nurturing, harvesting, and preparation of herbs for ritualistic use. However, here are some common herbs you might find in starter kits and their intended usage:

- **Alfalfa:** This herb is used in spells that are meant to protect the caster from poverty and hunger. While it could be considered a herb used for prosperity spells, the herb is mostly specialized in spells combating poverty and hunger specifically.
- **Bay Leaf**: These leaves are used in spells relating to cleansing a space of negative energy. It can also be used to invoke prophetic dreams when placed under a pillow.
- **Catnip:** This plant's relationship with cats makes it a perfect component for spells concerning cats. However, it can also be used in spells meant to improve mood, beauty, and love.
- **Comfrey:** This herb is used in spells meant to protect oneself during travel. This is most often done by wearing the plant or putting a bit of it in one's luggage to protect

it. It can also be used in spells dealing with money, primarily when land is involved. However, never put comfrey in your mouth. The plant is highly toxic and has the potential to cause liver failure.

- **Dandelions:** This plant actually has different uses depending on which part you use. The roots are often associated with protection from nightmares and are used in spells for spiritual assistance. The leaves are used in spells meant to fight off and heal the effects caused by negativity.

- **Eucalyptus:** The leaves of this plant are used for healing spells and spells used to maintain health. This extends to mental and emotional health, and it can aid in resolving personal conflicts when placed inside an amulet. That being said, you shouldn't consume the leaves. The herb is toxic and can result in horrible side effects if ingested.

- **Hyssop:** Considered to be one of the most potent purification herbs, this plant is often used to clean a caster's temple, tools, and the caster themselves. It can also be hung around the home to cleanse a space of negativity and ill intent.

- **Lavender:** This flower is used in a whole range of spells, from offering pleasant sleep to healing negative wounds. The herb is also known to bring peace and harmony within one's home and oneself. It can also be used in love spells.

- **Mint:** This plant is often used in spells involving protection, healing, and increasing wealth.

- **Mugwort:** This plant is used primarily in divination, either it be through visions or dreams. This can either be used directly in a spell or used to cleanse or empower other materials used in such spells. When carried, the herb is said to increase lust, fertility, mental wellness and physical wellness.

- **Nettle:** The leaves of this plant are used to remove morbid thoughts and fears from one's mind and to strengthen the will of the caster. Spells using this herb are meant to aid a person deal with stressful or dangerous situations.

- **Peppermint:** This herb can be used as incense to heal a home of sickness and negative energy. However, the true strength of peppermint lies with its power to boost the strength of other spells. Specifically, spells involving love and abundance. This is commonly done by wearing peppermint along with other herbs.

- **Rose:** The petals of this flower are used in spells focused on love and relationships. These relationships don't have to be romantic in nature, but the spells using roses are meant to create a lasting bond between two people.

- **Rosemary:** This herb is often worn to improve a person's memory. It can also be burned to purify a home of negativity and is often used in an infusion to purify one's hands in order to strengthen healing spells. You shouldn't consume the plant at any time as it is toxic to humans.

- **Sage:** The leaves of this plant are used for personal purification and overall increase in a person's wellbeing. It also repels negative energy associated with grief and loss. A special use of this herb is for a wish granting ritual. By writing a desire on a leaf and placing it under a pillow, the wish will come true if the caster dreams of their wish for three nights in a row.

- **St. John's Wort**: This herb is used in protection and banishing spells aimed at blocking out negative or evil energy. Is also used for simple rituals such as being worn to protect the wearer from cold or fevers. A quick disclaimer is that this herb can be poisonous if consumed in moderate amounts. It can also cause sun sensitivity if it makes contact with skin. Handle this herb with care.

- **Yarrow:** This flower is often associated with love and marriage, and most spells using it pertain to such. Some claim that making a marriage sachet or charm using a yarrow keeps a marriage standing for seven years by protecting the couple from harmful influences. Other spells using yarrow focus on inspiring courage and confidence within the user, allowing them to face their fears.

While this is not a complete list, this should be enough for you to understand what the materials within a starting kit are meant for. Additionally, this should also show that some of the plants used for rituals are dangerous if consumed and some may be dangerous to rub on oneself. If you don't know if a plant is safe or not, don't put it in your mouth, even if a ritual has it as one of its steps.

Other Items

The basic components of spells are good on their own for certain rituals. However, there are other tools of the trade that might be needed depending on the spell's purpose. Some items all casters need is a ceremonial knife, a small knife meant to cut herbs, and a fireproof bowl. The second and third one is for practical reasons, as you might not want to use the same knives used for cooking food on your herbs, or vice versa, and rituals involving fire can be dangerous if not isolated in a fireproof item. The ceremonial knife may seem nefarious to some. Remember though, this isn't a movie. The knife isn't used for cutting in the majority of spells, but instead is used as a symbol for something else.

While certain components are meant to aid in divination, the heavy lifters of this practice are often something else. Tarot cards, runes, and scrying all are used for divination, so spells conducting such acts usually involve one of them. Tarot cards are the most popular of these forms of divination, and it is easy to see why. Not only are they easy to understand, but there are also many versions of tarot cards that it is easy to make a collection out of the various iterations.

Runes and scrying are less popular ways of looking into the future. Runes are symbols placed on a certain material (usually stone) that are shuffled and tossed. Where and how they land is then used to make predictions about the future. Scrying is a bit more complex to explain as there are many methods one can conduct scrying. However, unlike rune reading and tarot cards, scrying usually involves one or two objects handled in a way to invoke prophetic readings.

Another item that might be needed is a wand of some kind. If you remember earlier, this book previously poked fun at the fact most media portrays wands making magic appear out of thin air. That criticism still stands. Wands do not spew out magic like a firework display. Instead, the wand serves a purpose akin to the ceremonial knife; it is a symbol. However, acquiring a wand can be tricky, as many claim the most potent wands are the ones you make yourself. As this guide is for beginners, it is not recommended you try making a wand for your first spell. Get a handle on your magick before making one, as the wand itself has no magickal properties of its own.

Finally, once you wish to expand your knowledge even further, it will be time for you to get more books on the subject of magick and spells. Or, if you want to experiment a bit, having a journal recording what you find works best for you is a good idea to keep track of your findings. Both may be needed in the future, especially if you want to recall a ritual that worked well for you before. Keeping track this way also enables you to know which components you need to stock up on.

CHAPTER 3
PREPARATION

Once all materials are gathered, the next step is to prepare the casting of the spell. Preparation can be an entire task in itself depending on the specificity of the spell. Certain spells require a specific location or time of day in order to work. Additionally, the date itself may hold importance for the ritual to be successful. For example, during a full moon, many believe that energy coming from the Moon is at its strongest. To capture this increase in energy, some place jars of clean water in a location exposed to the moon in order to absorb some of the energy it transmits. This exposure leads to the creation of moon water, which can be used for healing spells, a cleansing ritual, or just general use.

If there isn't a location specified for the best results from a spell, you can conduct it in any place that is quiet where you can concentrate.

However, even if a spell doesn't have a specific

location, spells typically work better if the location reflects the target of your spell. If your spell is about yourself or another person, being indoors may make more sense. The spell could be further strengthened if the room is significant for the target of the spell, such as a room they have a fondness for. Alternatively, if the spell is associated with nature and animals, casting the spell outdoors may make more sense, with the environment surrounding the caster reflecting the target's natural environment. For example, if the spell is for the wellness of a pet turtle, a lake or pond would be preferable over a forest or an open plain.

Once you know when and where you want to cast the spell, the next step is considering the spell's true intention. While you may have a general idea about what type of spell you want to cast, you will need to have a focused intention when you cast it. Having it written down somewhere or affirming to yourself that this is what you want out of the spell will help keep it focused when you actually cast it. However, while it should be focused, it shouldn't be specific. Spells are generally not powerful enough to alter the world in precise ways. Spells influence the world as it stands instead of bending reality to fit a person's intentions. If you want the spell to give you $3000 over the span of three days by having someone pay you $1000 each day, the spell will not work because that small influence would have to shift too many things. Instead, have the spell's intention be something more general.

CHAPTER 4
CONDUCTING THE RITUAL

Due to the wide variety of spells, trying to declare an exact way to conduct one is hard to do. Some spells have spoken parts, so making sure you have a clear throat is important. Other times, spells require the caster or casters to move around. In such instances, having enough room to conduct the spell is important. Most spells require high concentration, so making sure you aren't interrupted or distracted is also important. In some ways, casting a spell is the easiest part. If you are following the instructions of another caster, it should be easy as long as everything is set up correctly. If you are attempting to cast a spell of your own creation, it would be better if you wrote the instructions down beforehand in preparation of finally casting it.

A standard step in many spells that could be

taken, but is not required, is to make a magick circle. A magick circle is intended to boost one's spell in exchange for additional preparation. In order to create one, you need a purification tool or spell ready, something to form the circle, and the items you need for the other spell you want to cast. Start by purifying the room you wish to cast the spell in. This cleanses the room of negative energy so the circle can amplify positive energy. Then place the items you need for the other spell in the center of where you want your circle to be. This works as an altar, with your intentions being forced onto that central point. After everything is in place, form the circle. This can be done by drawing on the floor or placing items around the perimeter of the desired circle. Limit the material used to something that can be easy to clean, as the circle must be broken at the end ritual in order to work. If you are conducting the spell outside, natural objects like sticks and stones can work to form the circle. Just make sure there is enough room for you to be inside the circle when you are done forming it.

When conducting a ritual, never end the casting prematurely or get distracted. The spell will fail and you will have to start the process all over again. Additionally, there is a chance that the spell may backfire if it is interrupted. If it does, don't worry. You won't find yourself in a movie plot where you are targeted by vengeful spirits or demons. Most likely, it will just cause some minor inconvenience to occur. Still, to stop yourself from repeating a spell's process over and over again, ensure you are comfortable before casting a spell. This is especially true if you are conducting the spell outside, as being too hot or too cold can ruin concentration. On the day you plan on conducting a spell outside, check weather reports before properly dressing for the ritual. Remember, the best way to cast a spell is to focus on your intentions and remove as many distractions as possible.

Once the spell is completed, clean up and simply wait for the results or cast another spell. It may take some time for the spell to come to fruition, so don't expect immediate results. While repeated casting may strengthen it, casting the same spell multiple times on the same day will not result in any noticeable differences. Give it some time before trying the same spell again. If you have a magick circle, make sure to break it during cleanup. Magick circles buildup energy, so not breaking the circle keeps the spell's energy locked within that space.

If you wish to cast more than one spell, make

sure they don't conflict with one another while casting inside a magick circle. Conflicting intentions may result in nothing happening or some middle ground that weakens both spells.  Even if you think the two spells don't contradict, it may be safer to simply finish the process of one spell, break the circle, then wait a minute or two before doing the second one. Even if you aren't casting in a magick circle, it may be better to keep two spells about vastly different things away from each other. Two conflicting spells may result in something neither intended.

CHAPTER 5
SPELLS

As mentioned throughout this book, there are many types of spells one can cast. Just like their components, these types vary from each other and some are casted differently than the vast majority of spells. Additionally, some types of spells have more power than others depending on their relationship with the natural world. Magick is usually associated with universal energy, something that is not inherently part of man-made designs. Due to this, spells concerning man-made items or structures may not be as effective when compared to naturalistic spells. This doesn't make those types of spells worthless, but it does mean spells asking for material things or status are relatively weaker compared to spells that aim at performance, emotion, or one's environment.

Purification Spells

The only spell that never needs a magick circle, purification spells are counters to ill intents, negativity, and dark spirits. The actual target of these spells can vary from small items to large rooms to even people. There is no way such spells can backfire as their purpose is to remove negative elements from a person, space, or object. If the spell fails, it most likely just means the caster will have to try again.

The only restriction that is associated with these types of spells is that you will most likely have to be near the target of the spell in order for it to work the best. Unlike other spells, purification spells don't typically work indirectly. When you cleanse something, it is cleansed almost immediately. This immediate result has the trade-off that the range of the spell is severely limited. Think of it like an explosion. Purification spells have an explosive amount of energy, removing all negativity from the vicinity. The further away something is, the less likely the explosion will be effective.

There is one subject that is a point of contention when it comes to purification spells. That point is the question if purification spells or healing spells should be used to help treat disease. There is no clear answer to that question, as some claim that purification spells help while others claim that healing spells are better. While neither are a replacement for medicine, it is still an argument one can have when it comes to spell choice. In addition, due to the complex nature of humans, purification spells may have a harder time removing negative thoughts from a person. For example, if you cast a purification spell at a pessimist with an aim to remove that person's negativity, that pessimist will not be affected as that negativity is part of that person's pessimistic personality.

Healing Spells

Healing spells are targeted at healing the body, mind, spirit, or a combination of the three. It should be clear that these aren't a full replacement for medical or psychological help. No spell is powerful enough to alter the body or mind in that way. What they can do is provide relief, comfort, and aid in the healing process. While they might not be powerful enough to cure an illness, they can be the tipping point that allows someone to recover faster.

The materials used in healing spells change a bit depending on what you want to heal. For example, if you wish to heal someone's spirit, you might want to use a purple candle due to their spiritual significance. For the body, a red candle is more appropriate as they are used in spells associated with physical performance, which includes a body's natural inclination to heal itself. Think about what you intend to heal with this spell and base your materials off that aspect.

Protection Spells

Protection spells are similar to healing spells as they can be applied to the body, mind, and spirit. However, unlike healing spells, protection spells can also be applied to places and objects. Additionally, unlike healing spells, which only deal with the aftermath of an issue, protection spells are meant to prevent bad things from occurring.

Even if a bad thing does happen, protection spells still lessen the impact of the event to reduce the amount of harm done.

Like other spells, protection spells can also have a delayed effect. Let's say you plan on traveling and you wish to feel a bit more secure in your travels. Casting a protection spell can help protect you on your travels before you even go on it. That being said, there isn't a noticable difference between a spell aimed at a later date and a spell done at the same time as the action. In other words, if you forget to cast a protection spell before doing something, you can still cast it to get the same amount of protection from it. As long as the ritual is properly done, a caster should get the same amount of protection from a spell every time.

Love Spells

As mentioned previously, magick can't control minds. Fictional stories regularly paint love spells or potions as this, even if the use of it is supposed to be "funny." True love spells don't work like that. Love spells actually come in two types: discover love spells and strengthen love spells.

Discover love spells are spells focused on finding a companion. While this doesn't have to be a romantic partner, it most often is, though there are spells out there aimed at finding new friends. Discover love spells are like bird calls: they are signals aimed at helping the speaker (or caster in this case) find a partner. If you are on dating apps or similar services, the change will probably be unnoticable. These spells focus on helping you discover possible connections with the people around you. If you are seeking a romantic partner while using dating services, you are already seeking to find these connections. Sending out more signals isn't going to help that much.

Even if you have no use for discovering love spells, most people can find use in strengthening love spells. Strengthening love spells are spells focused on bolstering the bonds between two people. The bond doesn't have to be romantic, but it is recommended that both parties within the relationship are present for the spell. If both are present and accepting of the spell's power, the spell itself will become more powerful compared to ones done by only one person in the relationship. Even if only one person of the relationship is casting, both sides have to be receptive to the spell's intentions. If the person targeted by the spell doesn't want to have a strengthened bond with the caster, or vice versa, the spell will not work.

Prosperity Spells

Prosperity spells are an umbrella term for spells that are meant to increase an aspect of life. This is intentionally vague as what that thing is depends on the spell. For example, some spells focus on increasing fertility or aiding the growth of plants while other spells focus on financial gain. These spells focus on physical parts of life either by directly providing the requested goods or by influencing factors to increase the probability of gaining what one desires. These spells are technically the weakest type of spells.

Unlike other spells that influence things on their own or help benefit preexisting systems, prosperity spells require the caster to do something to aid it after casting it. For example, if the caster casted a spell to increase their harvest and do nothing to tend to their plants, the spell will not work as the plants the spell was aimed at weren't properly cared for. In order to get the most out of the spell, the caster would still need to take care of the plants. Prosperity spells work on future actions, not actions of the present or the past. This makes them the weakest as their effect may hardly be noticeable depending on the target of the spell.

Invigoration Spells

Invigoration spells is an umbrella term for spells that are meant to boost an aspect of oneself. This could be anything from energy to mood to creativity to even physical performance. These spells help the caster gain focus and clarity while also allowing them to push their body to the limits. Like with healing spells, these types of spells change depending on the materials used to cast them. If you want to boost more than one aspect of yourself, you will need materials reflecting both aspects you wish to increase.

A thing to note is that invigoration spells don't add anything. They simply reveal what doubt hides and releases the true strength that lies within the caster. So no, these spells do not replace workouts, study habits, or good diets. They only allow the caster to work with all they have, something that life can cloud through everyday problems. While some may argue that invigoration spells are weaker than prosperity spells, the truth is that doubts and a lack of confidence can be very detrimental to performance. Having something to boost confidence can provide an immediate and noticeable improvement compared to spells that may have effects that aren't noticeable.

Divination Spells

Divination spells are focused on gaining new insights about yourself or the world around you. While this can be about the future, divination spells do not need to focus on it. They could help figure out one's current relationship with a coworker or they can help provide a new perspective on a recent event. Divination is simply aimed at exploring the unknown, with the spells associated with it aimed at answering the mysteries the unknown holds.

As mentioned previously, divination spells have their own unique materials such as tarot cards and rune stones. However, they are not the only materials used for divination spells, so solely relying on them can be very limiting. Take tarot cards for example. While they can brush upon a person's past, present, and future, they can't focus on any one thing. They can give general observations and allow one to reassess their knowledge on certain events, but they don't target events directly. While there are other spells that can do that, tarot readings aren't as focused as one might wish them to be.

Tarot Cards

Tarot card readings are often the poster child of divination. There are many ways to use tarot cards for divination with the most commonly portrayed method being a three card spread  where the past, present, and future are laid out in front of you. However, despite this popular picture, tarot cards are a bit more complicated than that. This is not simply because there are techniques that use more than three cards, but because those readings solely use the major arcana cards.

A full tarot card set includes seventy-eight cards, twenty-two belonging to the major arcana while fifty-six belong to the minor arcana. Major arcana are the most popular and most impactful cards. These cards are meant for large scale questions about one's personal life and one's potential future. Unlike the minor arcana, the major arcana all have their own individual names, such as "The Hermit," "The Hanged Man," and "The World." While some have similarities, all of the major arcana cards are seen as their own entities and are only grouped together due to their importance.

The minor arcana is something you don't see

a lot in the media. Like a set of playing cards, the minor arcana is divided into four groups. While their names can be different depending on the set you are using, the original and standard names for them are wands, cups, swords, and pentacles. These sets, following the same number and name system as a regular deck, are meant to answer more day-to-day questions and minor concerns. Each set deals with a different aspect of one's life, with each card relating to their set's meaning. Wands focus on creativity and ambition, cups are focused on emotions and relationships, swords focus on intuition and finding truth, and pentacles focus on material things and ways to get them. Major and minor arcana can be used together in certain readings, but there are plenty that just focus on one and not the other.

Rune Reading

Rune divination spells are not as popular as tarot cards but can still be used to answer questions or make predictions of the future. The most popular form of rune reading is based on the Norse runic alphabet, which consists of 24 symbols, each with their own meaning. While some symbols may seem odd to certain people, others are very similar or exact copies of letters found in the Latin alphabet. For example, there is an "X" and an "R" in the Norse runic alphabet. Each of these has a secondary name attached to them, with "X" having the name "Gebo" and "R" having the name "Raidho."

Divination using rune stones comes in a variety of ways, though the simplest is by using only one rune. The way to conduct this form of divination is by first getting a bag full of the runes and shaking it in one hand. Carefully consider the question you wish to answer before putting your hand in the bag. Without looking, pick out a stone that feels right to pull out. Once you pull it out, notice everything about the rune. Was the rune facing you when you pulled it out? Was the rune upside down? Once you take note of how it was pulled out, reference the rune's meaning in order to make an interpretation about what the rune meant in relation to your question.

That is one method of using runes for divination. Some rituals use multiple runes, either by tossing the stones out of the bag onto a soft surface or by pulling out multiple stones. However, like tarot cards, the answers aren't always clear. Runes have multiple meanings. On top of that, while they can be described with common themes, their direct translation can be vague.

For example, Raidho can be interpreted as road or journey. While this may seem obvious in many contexts, you might be confused if you pulled the rune out after asking whether or not someone is into you. Assuming you pulled the rune out while it was facing you and it was right-side up, it could mean that the relationship will be a journey with no clear way of telling whether or not it will end the way you want it. Alternatively, it could mean that the roads the two of you walk on may be parallel, meaning the two of you may not get into a romantic relationship, but a platonic one. Both interpretations are valid, even though they contradict.

Scrying

Scrying is difficult to explain because there are multiple methods one can do in order to scry. Some look into flames for messages while others use a crystal ball or other reflective surface to look for visions. Of the several types, looking into reflective surfaces is considered the most popular and easiest to do. However, no matter what method one takes in order to scry, there are similarities in all scrying spells.

Firstly, like with other spells, scrying requires that the practitioner isn't interrupted. Unlike tarot and rune reading however, scrying can be a very lengthy process. While the other two already discussed forms of divination could reach up to half an hour per session, it is very rare for that to happen. For scrying, thirty minutes may be a little longer than usual, but it shouldn't be unexpected. The reason why is because scrying requires the caster to be in a meditative state. In order for one to properly scry, one has to be in a calm, relaxed state of being. Even once someone is in that state of being, it may take time before the material used actually shows an image or message.

Of course, simply being in a meditative state doesn't help answer a question. To attain visions that answer their question, the caster needs to think about the topic they want answers to while gazing into the object. The way one actually looks at the object shifts from item to item, with some items requiring clear vision while others require the caster to watch with an unfocused stare. Some scrying even requires the caster to observe the exact details of an object to make predictions, though these processes are a bit more advanced. Record your observations and try to interpret what the signs mean once the scrying is complete for the best results.

CHAPTER 6
SPELLCRAFTING

All this information means little if we can't cast a spell ourselves. There are dozens of books filled to the brim with spells, some larger than others. However, since an important part of the craft is making your own spells, this book shall go through the method one can take to make a spell. There will also be an example, as no book about spells isn't complete without having one itself.

Step 1: Determining What You Want

As with all spells, the reason why you want to cast it is because you want something. It doesn't have to be selfish. However, each spell has a desire behind it, and the first step is finding out which one you want to impose. Perhaps you have a sick family member and wish to make them better. A

healing spell would work best for you in that case. Maybe you have a rough presentation to show tomorrow, and you want to spend the night practicing to make sure you get it right. An invigoration spell can aid you in focusing on your practice.

While this may seem like a simple step, it is very important you know for sure what you want.

Magick and spells reflect the intentions of the caster. If the caster doesn't want the effects of the spell to take hold, either consciously or subconsciously, the spell will most likely fail as the caster wasn't dedicated to the spell's intentions. They don't need to be devoted to the spell, but they should think carefully about whether or not they want what they think they want.

For the purposes of this book, let us make a simple protection spell aimed at keeping us safe at night from burglars.

Step 2: Gathering the Appropriate Material

As mentioned before, most spells have material in one form or another. Making sure you have the right material is important for any caster. This step is basically just the application of Chapter 2, so just use that for reference. That being said, just because a piece of material is meant to aid in a certain type of spell doesn't mean you need that material. In fact, if you believe the spell you wish to cast doesn't need materials, you can skip this step entirely.

For our example, materials will be used just to show how they can be incorporated into a spell. The protection spell shall use a brown or white candle as the main component. Brown due to the earthly nature of this protection and white because that color of candle can take the place of any other candle.

Step 3: Planning Out the Ritual

This is when we decide a time and place to conduct the ritual. Additionally, this is when we write up an incantation to use to help focus our intention towards the spell. This incantation could either be verbal or mentally spoken, but it should be written down for reference. While the time or place could be flexible, the invocation itself should be pretty strict. The strictness helps keep focus, which is important for any spell.

For our protection spell, the invocation shall be, "Of this room, none shall be taken. Of this space, no intruder shall enter. Of my home, let no crime happen."

Step 4: Testing a Spell

Finally, once that is all done, it is time to test the spell. How you test it really depends on what you want out of the spell. Are you searching for love? Then you most likely would just stay in one room. Are you trying to purify the house? Then perhaps moving through several rooms is appropriate. Is the spell targeted at someone? Then you might want to have a picture or object associated with that person. There isn't really a guide on how to test a spell as it really depends on what *you* think is needed for it.

For the protection spell, since it is to protect the home from burglars, the spell itself will be tested by moving from room to room reciting the incantation.

Step 5: Sharing the Spell

While this step isn't required, you might want to write down and share your spell with other people. Do know if you do this people are going to have mixed reactions. Some will be skeptical, others will be outright dismissive, but there will be those truly interested in the spell you've crafted. As long as you stay respectful and safe, there shouldn't be any problems with sharing your spell.

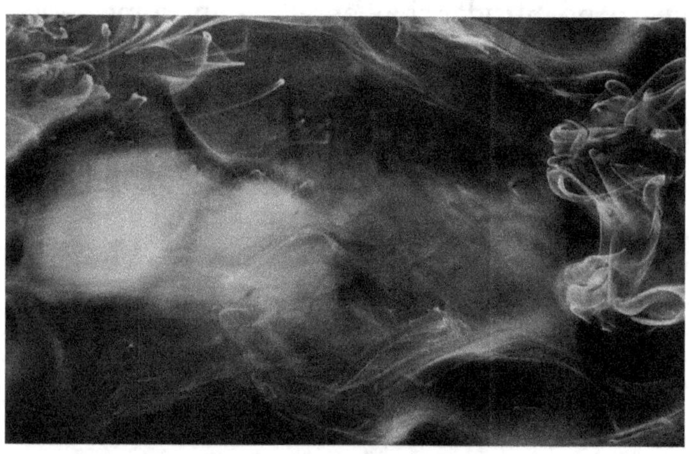

If you want an example of how to format your

spell, here is one way to do it:

Protection From Burglars Spell

During sunset, ignite a brown candle in the furthest room of your house. Recite the following:

"Of this room, none shall be taken. Of this space, no intruder shall enter. Of my home, let no crime happen."

Walk through each room you wish to protect while reciting the phrase, making sure to repeat each time you enter a room you haven't walked through before. Once you reach your front door, blow out the candle and set it down on the floor.

This is only an example and really you can format the written form of the spell in any way you think is most appropriate.

CHAPTER 7
ALTERNATIVE MAGICK

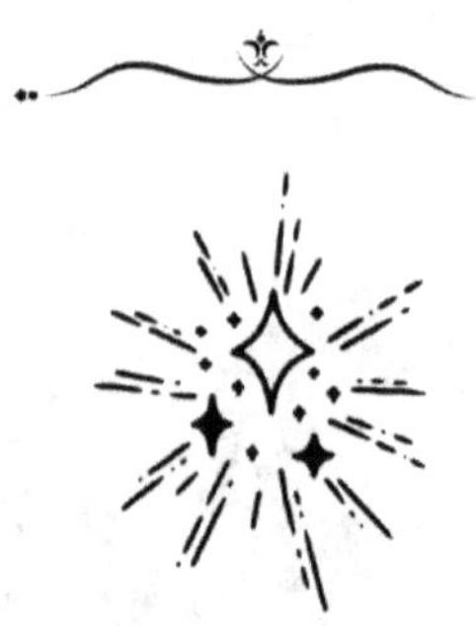

As stated earlier, most of the magick described in this book involves the practice of Wicca. However, there are several more types of magickal practices out there. From old practices such as Druidism and Heka to modern structures such as Satanism and Thelema Magick, there are those who conduct magick rituals while not directly associating themselves with Wiccans. Some of these practices have been abandoned, while others have many practitioners in the modern-day. These practices are varied in both history and techniques, as well as what their magick is intended for.

Druidism

Druidism is unique when it comes to fictional depictions. Unlike generic magic, several fictional settings distinguish Druidism as its own thing entirely, treating the group of practitioners differently from other spellcasters. Additionally, while wizards and witches are depicted in numerous ways, Druids are usually restricted to magic related to nature. This includes such things as shapeshifting into an animal and asking nature spirits to aid them in battle. While the literal interpretations and dramatization of such powers are to be expected, the core ideas in fictional Druidism are surprisingly accurate to modern Druidic practices.

"Modern" is the key word that needs to be focused on when talking about Druidism. The Celtic origins of this form of magick lacks written records, meaning all information pertaining to them are either from secondhand accounts or from testimonies of those who keep up the oral tradition of teaching the practice to younger generations. Additionally, like other types of ancient magick discussed later on, there was no unified version of Druidism. While there will still be plenty of discussion about Druidic beliefs, like Wiccans, Druidism is a complex and branching topic that has different interpretations. Additionally, while Wiccans and Druids can be similar in many aspects, the two aren't inherently the same.

While the particulars of Druidism may shift

from group to group, there are some overarching themes present in all of them. Druidism regularly focuses on nature and the wisdom it provides, though how this wisdom is granted varies slightly between interpretations. Sometimes, the wisdom comes from nature spirits. Other times, it is from gods and goddesses. How this wisdom is given is usually consistent, though, with the seeker communing with the giver in a natural setting.

Druidism treats nature differently though from most modern perceptions. Instead of acting as if nature is one unified unit, Druidism is based on regional power. For instance, the wisdom and power present in one forest may not be the same for another forest several miles away, as the needs and ecological balance of these forests could be different in nature. Due to this regional focus, one could argue that even in heavily populated cities one could find nature's wisdom, though it would be harder to do as nature isn't as prominent there.

Another thing that many Druids conduct is the celebration of the solstices and equinoxes as well as four seasonal holidays. One of the more famous of the seasonal holidays is Samhain, as it is on the same day as Halloween. This is no coincidence, as Samhain merged with another holiday, All Hallows' Eve, to become Halloween, with Samhain's influences being seen through the traditions of costume-wearing and trick-or-treating (History.com Editors, 2018a). Other holidays include Imbolc at the start of spring, Beltane at the start of summer, and Lammas near the beginning of autumn. The specific dates for these holidays aren't as clear as Samhain's, which adds further confusion when taking the hemispheres into account.

Other than that, Druidism doesn't really have unifying details, even in its earliest days. Welsh, Scottish, and Irish practitioners all had minor differences between them. While the most obvious would be their location, different terminology was also used between the three groups. For example, some Scottish Druids called spirits or fairies "devils," though they weren't associated with the Christian concept of a devil (Forest, 2020). This expectantly didn't go down well with Christain missionaries, leading to certain Druid groups being accused of malicious witchcraft (Forest, 2020). Additionally, experts of local Druidic practices were called different names. In certain parts of Ireland, Druidic medical experts were called *bean feasa* or "wise-women," while in Britain, they were called

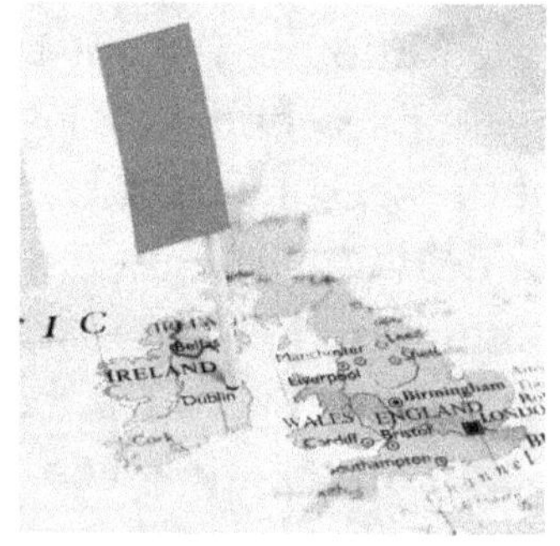

"the cunning folk" (Forest, 2020).

On top of different terminology, they also faced different levels of discrimination when engaged with Christians. As stated previously, Scottish Druids calling helpful fairies "devils" caused several of these groups to be persecuted. However, in Wales and Ireland, this problem did not arise as often, with their magick actually being seen as an important part of many local communities (Forest, 2020). Thanks to such groups surviving, modern-day Druidic groups have an easier way to trace back their practices and historians have a better chance to understand Druidic beliefs, though there is still a large lack of historical Druidic records.

The idea of a Druidic group existing in the modern-day may seem like a surprise to some, but the fact is that multiple organizations practicing Druidism exist. One group, the Order of Bards, Ovates, and Druids (OBOD) are based in England and are considered by some to be the largest of these modern groups. The OBOD's website offers more in-depth teachings of Druidry and even offers members the ability to become a "celebrant," a priest of sorts who is "able to design and lead Weddings/Handfastings, Funerals, Baby Namings & other Rites of Passage" (*Our Courses and Membership*, n.d.). Another modern group of

Druids is Ár nDraíocht Féin (ADF), an organization based in the United States. In Irish, the name means "our own magic," though they claim they "incorporate practices from ancient and modern Indo-European cultures including the traditions of Celtic and Norse cultures, Slavic, Baltic, Greek, Roman, Persian, Vedic, and other cultures" (*Ár nDraíocht Féin – Our Own Druidry*, 2022).

However, even in the modern-day, organizations have difficulty agreeing on what defines Druidism. The OBOD considers Druidism to be a loose term that could mean religion, spiritual path, or simply a philosophy. However, the ADF explicitly calls themselves a church, making their view on Druidism different from the OBOD's.

With all that in mind, one might find it hard to actually figure out what would constitute a Druid spell. Fortunately, there are plenty of examples that one can work with. One practice was the memorization and use of hymns, chants, and incantations in a particular verse structure. Ancient Irish Druids used this practice, calling such songs and poems *cetal* or *laedha* structured (Maccrossan, 2002). Poetic language itself, either sung or simply stated, carries the magick in this situation, with the words chosen to create a specific effect. Another thing Irish poets used were "ogams; numerals, ciphers and codes made from notches carved along the straight edge of a twig" meant for divination purposes (Maccrossan, 2002).

Something that fantasy Druids and actual Druids do share is the ability to alter themselves to become an animal. For fantasy Druids, this is

literally interpreted as the ability to shapeshift. For real Druids, the rituals and incantations used to invoke this ability alters the mindset of the caster and doesn't actually cause a physical transformation as radical as their fictional counterparts. Real Druids also tend to have more complex rituals. An example of this comes from a healing spell, where a caster dips a rag or clootie in a clean, blessed body of water before washing a sick person with the blessed rag, asking water spirits to bless and cure the ill person (Forest, 2020). The cloth is then hung from a tree, preferably a hawthorn, and left to rot, with the sickness being taken away as the rag decays (Forest, 2020).

While there are many rituals asking nature for aid, the relationship between Druids and nature isn't one-sided. Asking help from nature while neglecting or destroying it often results in a lot of failed spells. A Druid must have a strong, or at least decent, connection with nature, honoring it and asking for aid only when needed. However, beyond not littering and planting trees, there are other ways to become more connected with the land. Altars are a popular choice, as is meditation. Unlike some fictional depictions, the use of technology isn't directly harmful to one's relationship with nature. However, overusing or mishandling technology can weaken one's relationship, such as driving somewhere all the time when you can easily walk to the location. Balance is the key here.

Some may claim that Druid spells and Wicca spells are interchangeable to some extent. To be fair, they are right. Many of the tools, herbs, and methods used to cast Wiccan spells would still find some use in a pure Druidic practice. However, what makes Druids unique is the fact that a Druid never needs to cast a spell to be considered a Druid. Spells aren't required for those who follow the tenets of Druidism, hence why the OBOD recognizes that some people who call themselves Druids simply see it as a philosophy. Not every Druid practices with magick in mind, so even if you aren't interested in or believe in Druidic spells, you could be interested in the more complex nature of Druidic belief.

Heka

Heka is the Egyptian form of magick that draws origins from the god Heka. Due to the nature of Heka, the magick associated with it is directly connected to the old Egyptian deities. Despite this being a very old form of magick, many of the rituals conducted through Heka have similar modern-day examples. Some have argued that Heka has inspired modern-day magic and magick in various ways. Being one of the oldest practices out there, it would make sense if this is true.

One aspect of Heka that is seen in most modern interpretations of magick is the belief that everyone has access to it. While priests and doctors were the primary authorities for the practice, Ancient Egyptian lifestyle catered to the concept that everyone could invoke the power

Heka provides. The most common application of this was to wear amulets, which are akin to modern-day charms. These charms were usually meant for protection, though they could be used to invoke other qualities. Additionally, Egyptian Heka might have inspired the eventual popularization of connecting wands to magic, as ivory wands were used during stressful times.

Something that bleeds into popular media depictions of spellcraft from Heka is the importance of pronunciation. According to Dr. Geraldine Pinch, in order for a spell to work, "all the words, especially the secret names of deities, had to be pronounced correctly" (Pinch, 2011). While this idea does apply to other practices of magick, this concept is more prevalent in media, where magic is more likely to go wild if the speaker mispronounces a word. However, unlike popular media, Dr. Pinch goes further and details that, "Many spells included speeches, which the doctor or the patient recited in order to identify themselves with characters in Egyptian myth" (Pinch, 2011). The purpose of these speech spells were meant to help manifest an outcome similar to the nature of the myth recited. As stated in the quote, this type of ritual was primarily incorporated into healing spells conducted by doctors.

Speaking of healing magick, one might improperly assume that, due to the nature of Heka, the Egyptians would use only spells to deal with illnesses while ignoring medicine. Nothing could be further from the truth. Ancient Egyptian doctors used a combination of healing spells and medical practices to help the ill and wounded. While they did believe evil spirits would cause the illness that must be repelled, they also recognized that such spells didn't stop the physical harm caused by such spirits.

What is unique for Heka compared to many forms of magick practice is that written magick is seen as a highly coveted item. Due to the low rate of literacy in Ancient Egypt, written spells were a rarity as only a select few could write them. This rarity doesn't necessarily make it more powerful. Instead, they were valued for their long-lasting effects. As stated previously, words have magick power in Heka, and this power wouldn't be diluted if it was written on paper. This meant that a written spell would last longer while still holding the strength of a standard ritual. These written spells were often seen as a more powerful alternative to amulets, with written spells being "handed down within families" in order to keep such strong magick on hand (Pinch, 2011).

Heka was a very important thing for Egyptians, even in death. Famously, the Egyptian *Book of the Dead* is filled with spells that were meant to protect a person as they traveled through the afterlife. However, while the popular fascination with mummies have helped bring such a text some popularity, the hyperfixation has limited people's knowledge on the day-to-day practices conducted by regular citizens. While the dead did practice Heka, they were just doing something that they had practiced while they were alive.

Kotodama

Kotodama is a unique form of magick for two

reasons. The first is that it is an entirely vocal and written form of magick, with the words themselves being the only thing that truly matters for this type of magick. The second is that it is directly tied to a language, specifically Japanese. Like other forms of magick, the origins of Kotodama are old. Unlike other forms though, Kotodama still has incredible influence over modern culture today in Japan. However, like many cultural things, Kotodama has changed over the centuries due to its connection with the Japanese language.

Before exploring that, we must first discuss what Kotodama is in terms of power. Like most forms of magick, everyone can do it as long as they can speak Japanese. Unlike most forms, additional training isn't required. Instead, the power results in the words you choose to use. According to Kotodama, saying or writing positive words result in positive results. Similarly, the use of negative words results in negative results. While some may associate Kotodama with karma, Kotodama differs in the fact that the target of the words receives the outcome of a person's word choice. If you speak positively about something, they receive a positive result instead of you, and vice versa. While this may all seem simple, the history surrounding what counts as Japanese makes this much harder to pin down.

The birth of Kotodama was caused by a fusion of Shinto, a religion that started in Japan, and *yamato kotoba*, the original language of Japan. In Shinto, it is believed that everything has a spirit attached to it, and this extends to words. In fact, Kotodama translates to the "spirit of language" or "power of language." Kotodama arose alongside Shintoism, with Shinto priests writing spells that sought for divine aid. However, like most languages, what was considered to be "Japanese" changed over time.

The earliest of these changes arrived during the introduction of Chinese words and elements. This form of Japanese, either called Sino-Japanese or *kango*, was created due to the major influence China had over its surrounding nations. While not a direct copy, *kango* added words that were either entirely Chinese or used elements from Chinese vocabulary. However, this adoption was seen as impure by the Shinto priests, who determined that only *yamato kotoba* was able to draw in the power of Kotodama. Despite this, *kango* was still adopted by many Japanese, which helps explain a major change that would happen to Kotodama.

During World War II, the Japanese government wished to strengthen nationalistic zeal in their country. One of the programs the government put in place was to reestablish Kotodama as a major force in Japanese life, claiming that traditional Japanese is, "at the core of the national unity and social virtue that is unique to Japan" (Hosokawa, 2014). However, despite claiming traditional Japanese was the key to unity, the Japanese at this time didn't stick with *yamato kotoba*. Instead, both *kango* and *yamato kotoba* were acceptable forms of Japanese in the eyes of the governing body, expanding the definition of what could be used in Kotodama.

This adoption wasn't entirely isolated though. Just like with Sino-Japanese words before, the Japanese government denounced the use of new words adopted from foreign territories. In this instance, the denounced words were *gairaigo*, words that came from or were heavily influenced by Western countries. Like *kango* words before them, *gairaigo* were seen as impure and therefore didn't have the power of Kotodama associated with them. Additionally, *gairaigo* words were replaced by Sino-Japanese words.

Kotodama is still culturally important to many

Japanese people. Many still connect Kotodama with unity, often using the concept to promote the exclusion of adopted or adoptable foreign words. On a smaller scale, people who believe in Kotodama usually have an aversion to negative words in certain social situations. A common example of this can be seen during weddings, where words that are associated with things ending or separating are avoided at all costs. Kotodama dictates that saying such words can lead to an ill marriage that results in divorce, so attendants at weddings avoid such words as much as possible. In fact, the belief is so strong that the end of a wedding is often called the "opening" (Geeraert, 2020).

Weddings are not the only instances where Kotodama can have a negative influence. During exams, words involving falling or an action that results in one falling are considered dangerous to say or write down as well. This is because literal translations of Japanese equate failing to falling in relation to tests, meaning that saying words associated with falling can result in influences that result in the tester failing (Geeraert, 2020).

Another thing affected by Kotodama is the reception of numbers. Due to pronunciation, certain numbers are often seen as unlucky due to a word or phrase that is close to the number's pronunciation. Some examples of negative words being associated with numbers include "stillbirth" with the number 43, "death" with the number 4, and "suffering" with the number 9. Due to the numbers being closely related to negative words, those who practice Kotodama usually avoid those numbers, especially in a hospital setting, so be careful when visiting Japan to not say negative or potentially harmful things. Words can be dangerous.

Mageia and Goeteia

Mageia or Goeteia, depending on the era in question, was the Greek term for magick. While both could apply to the Greek tradition of magick, the term "mageia" was actually derived from the Persian term *magos* (*Goêteia Explorations in Chthonic Sorcery*, n.d.). Of the two, Mageia is considered more popular in a historical context as social developments altered the Greek perspective on the subject of magick, partially when it was associated with goeteia (*Goêteia Explorations in Chthonic Sorcery*, n.d.). However, there seems to be no difference in the practice of either version, making it seem more like a branding decision than anything else.

Mageia practices were similar to many other practices in terms of what they were trying to accomplish. There are protection spells, luck spells, curative spells, and spells to increase one's fertility. The Greeks combined both inorganic materials, such as engraved amulets used for protection, and organic materials, such as flowers and plants to cure diseases. One of the most famous recorders of such information was Theophrastus, who was not only a philosopher, but also a botanist who made several observations and possible uses of plants. Some of these usages include getting rid of illness through the use of squill and to use early purple orchid as an aphrodisiac (Hayward, 2020).

(Statue of one of the father of bontany:
Theophrastus)

A large part of Greek Mageia was a type of practice many might find evil in modern contexts. Amongst the spells and protective amulets, the

Greeks also practice cursing to a certain extent. Greek curses usually came in the form of a tablet called a "katara." The curse was intended to weaken a rival or opponent. Additionally, there were figures called "kolossoi" that could be used in a similar manner.

There is a big difference between the two, however. Katara were entirely hostile, meaning that someone making or purchasing one was trying to settle a score. Namely, the power of the katara was to ask for aid from the underworld. By placing the katara in a grave or another hole that goes into the earth, the katara would request that agents from the underworld help harm a person in the living world. Kolossoi, while still being harmful to humans, were also used to bind evil spirits, weakening them in the process. This is because kolossoi are similar to the popular notion of a voodoo doll, though it would be wrong to say that kolossoi work in the exact same way. The most obvious difference between kolossoi and the popular imagination of a voodoo spell is that kolossoi can also target spiritual beings.

Despite not being as famous as other magick, Greeks still use some of the old symbols to this day. A prominent example of this is the evil eye, or *mati*, which is usually symbolized with a blue eye surrounded by a darker blue circle. An evil eye is a simple curse given to someone by way of a vengeful or hostile look that then translates to minor inconveniences for the recipient of the look. A way to counter the curse is to wear a symbol of mati on your person, mostly in the form of an amulet. There are other forms of protection against the evil eye, but an amulet is the most convenient as it doesn't require any additional action after putting it on. However, the evil eye is usually only a danger to those that are really vulnerable.

Mesopotamia Āšipūtu

This type of magick originates from Mesopotamia and, similar to Heka, is directly connected to Mesopotamian religious beliefs. Despite many magick practices being lost to time, Āšipūtu was able to survive thanks to the aid of cuneiform tablets. From those tablets, historians were able to discover an ancient form of magick, though the nature of it is a bit loose. Similar to Japanese Kotodama, Mesopotamian Āšipūtu changed as the civilization changed, though there are some things that are clear about the topic.

For starters, Āšipūtu was divided into four major types: "liminal magic" that was focused on changing a person or an object into something else, "defensive magic" that aimed to remove "an evil" from a targeted person, "aggressive magic" that was meant to increase one's "superiority, strength, and attractiveness," and "witchcraft," which in this case means a form of illegal magick that was meant to cause harm (Schwemer, 2014b). As one can already guess, witches in Mesopotamia have the same negative connotation as they had in several other civilizations in the past. However, unlike their later Christian counterparts, the treatment of witches was quite different.

While both Christians and Mesopotamians were more inclined to believe that women were more often witches, for the Mesopotamians, finding who that was wasn't important. Defensive magic didn't need the name of the witch to deflect harmful magic. In fact, evidence points that spells against witchcraft "emphasize that the identity of the evildoers is unknown to their innocent victim" (Schwemer, 2014a). Mesopotamian defensive spells designed to fight witchcraft regularly reflect the ill intent back on the hostile caster, potentially indicating that such spells work best if the victim of a hostile spell doesn't hold any hostility

towards a named individual in case they weren't the ones to cast the spell, but aggression was still held towards their assailant, even if their identity is supposed to be unknown. A common element for anti-witch spells is the destruction of a pair of figurines, one for a male, one for a female (Schwemer, 2014a). This destruction could include torturing the figurines as well, though the destruction was the final catalyst for the spell to take effect.

From this, one could assume that being a witch in this time period was completely safe. While it can be comparably safer compared to other regions, supposed witches could still be sentenced to death. However, the accuser was as in much danger as the accused. If the accuser had no proof that a person was a witch, the supposed witch would undergo a trial to prove their innocence (Schwemer, 2014a). If the accused passed their test, the accuser would be charged with the crime of falsely charging someone of ill deeds and punished accordingly. Unfortunately for the accuser, this most often resulted in death (Schwemer, 2014a). This controlled the number of witch trials, as the accuser was on trial just as much as the one they had accused.

However, so far, only the practitioners of illegal magick have been named. For legal practitioners, there were various names that correlated with their position in society. The āšipu, or ashipu, were the main practitioners of magick, holding a position akin to priests and exorcists. There was a group called the asu, or "physicians," that were similar to the ashipu that focused primarily on fixing illness and other maledictions (Said, 2018). There was also a separate group of divination practitioners called baru, who typically were in elite positions working directly under a king (Said, 2018). All of these practitioners were glorified in Mesopotamian society, though the baru stood out, as the ashipu and asu could take on each others' roles as needed.

Just like how modern historians are able to study Āšipūtu, it is theorized that the practitioners of old were taught through the use of cuneiform texts. This form of teaching allowed for standardization of spellcasting. Assyrians, who lived in Northern Mesopotamia, are a clear example of this standardization, as governing kings commanded the creation of a series of books referred to as "handbooks" to create a canonical and approved form of Āšipūtu (Said, 2018). However, even with this supposed standardization, there is some debate on how strictly these handbooks were practiced. Archeologists have discovered sites where the materials present seem to correspond with a ritual that doesn't perfectly match the phrasing of a cuneiform text about the same ritual (Mirelman,

2018). Sometimes, this variation is so extreme that entire objects used for ritualistic purposes were completely ignored. In one documented instance, ritualistic figurines were placed in "brick capsules," though the purpose of these capsules weren't detailed within a corresponding text (Mirelman, 2018). This gap in knowledge makes it hard for someone to create a modern version of the practice based primarily on historical evidence as there seems to be some variations between what was taught and what was practiced.

Even with these gaps, there are still commonalities that can be gained from the cuneiform texts and physical evidence. As

mentioned previously, defensive spells against witches regularly had figurines meant to depict the aggressor, but the use of figurines or similar objects were not limited to that single purpose, however. In fact, according to some researchers, Āšipūtu practitioners believed that images could have a will of their own, exerting such will by influencing the world around them (Said, 2018). An example of this comes in the form of the Iamassu, "massive, winged composite creatures with the head of a man and features of a bull or lion," that were built to guard important entryways from any form of metaphysical threat (Said, 2018). Unlike the figurines used in defensive spells, these statues were much larger, meaning that objects with magick came in a great variety of sizes for the Mesopotamians. However, there does seem to be a correlation with size and power when it comes to such objects.

While large statues made of stone were made to protect places of authority, people of lower social status could gain some protection through the use of guardian clay figures (Said, 2018). These protective idols came in a variety of shapes, though they were mostly "gods, animals, and hybrid creatures" (Said, 2018). Due to the difference in size and materials, it could be guessed that the larger and stronger a protective figure was, the greater the defense it could give against metaphysical threats. This difference in power did little in terms of placement, as even clay figures were put next to doorways and other places considered vulnerable to villainous spirits (Said, 2018). Upon reflection, one could see that the witch figurines that were meant to be destroyed during a defense ritual are an exception to an otherwise benevolent form of defense. This differentiation might be due to how Mesopotamians view illness in the first place.

Like the Egyptians, the Mesopotamians combined magick with medical practices to heal the sick and wounded. In fact, alongside their many cuneiform texts about casting away dark spirits, the Mesopotamians had a vast collection of medical texts, primarily in the form of pharmaceuticals (*Healing and Medicine: Healing and Medicine in the Ancient near East*, 2022). However, the Mesopotamians believed that the root cause of all misfortune and illnesses came from a personal lack of favor from the gods (*Healing and Medicine: Healing and Medicine in the Ancient near East*, 2022). The exact cause for this disfavor could be entirely unintentional, but because it still offended the gods, they would still seek retribution for that act. While demons and spirits could still inflict pain onto a person, it was only when they lost a god's favor was they became vulnerable to such attacks. If they had a god's favor, any metaphysical attack will fail thanks to divine protection. If we relate this back to the destruction of the witch figurines, it could be said that the destruction of such figures was to instill divine justice against those who had tried to take advantage of a person who needed to seek redemption.

Another common practice was the use of amulets and other accessories to protect one's body from malicious forces while outside of one's home. However, unlike the figurines and statues that resembled good deities and creatures,  amulets and pendants depicted dark deities and demons (Said, 2018). This was meant to deflect the evil entities, possibly working like a reflection to send such influence elsewhere. Other times, offerings to benevolent deities were marked around the symbol of the dark creature, neutralizing the dark force entirely (Said, 2018). Taking into account that people become vulnerable when they lose favor with the gods, perhaps the use of accessories in this way was meant to provide protection while still keeping face with protective deities. It could be interpreted that placing a divine being on an amulet means you want to drag them around everywhere, which could be seen as rude by divine beings. So instead of forcing the gods to follow them, the Mesopotamians chose to create barriers that could deflect or neutralize any negative force aimed at them.

So far, only defensive and witchcraft types of Āšipūtu magick has been talked about in length, and this isn't without reason. The other two major forms of Mesoptamain magick, liminal and aggressive, aren't the most pleasant to talk about. In fact, the latter of the two could be considered as bad, if not worse, than witchcraft. Aggressive spells that were completely legal at times included spells meant to charm the king, which could be used to gain political favors; forcing someone to fall in love, either with you or a person you know; and, probably worst of all, forcing a runaway slave to return to their master (Schwemer, 2014a). While these spells were sometimes grouped with other methods of witchcraft, the fact of the matter is that, at times, these spells were entirely legal to cast (Schwemer, 2014a). Only witchcraft was seen as illegal, so these spells that bordered between the two forms of legality shows how wicked even legal spells could be.

As mentioned earlier, though, most of the information found about Āšipūtu comes from historical texts. There aren't many, if any, modern-day practitioners, so it is hard to study modern practices. However, due to the Mesopotamian civilizations being considered the earliest in history, popular media likes to portray magic from the region in a similar way to witchcraft. This mostly comes through the "evil texts" or "evil idols" of the Sumerians, which were actually a group of people that resided in Mesopotamia. The truth is, while Āšipūtu did have spells that could be considered dark magick, the Sumerians and other Mesopotamians had a complex magick structure that wasn't entirely harmful, much less demonic. Their magick is certainly a morally questionable one, but not as bad as the movies make it out to be.

Obeah and Vodou

For witches, it can be argued that their existence was challenged by the ill will of humanity. For the Obeah and Vodou practitioners, the ill will of humanity brought them into existence. This is not because the two were created to do ill to others. It is because the suffering endured by the founders of the two was conducted by a cruel hand: a cruel hand most people know as the slave trade.

During the seventeenth century, the European powers, wishing to exploit the islands in the Caribbean, engaged in an African slave trade that displaced thousands of native Africans away from their homes. While the cruelties of this trade shouldn't be downplayed whatsoever, the focus of this book is not to criticize an inherently malicious practice. Instead, this book focuses on the new ideas that formed from such unfavorable conditions. Throughout the Caribbean, Africans from various ethnic groups came together to form diverse ideas. In Trinidad, the imported slaves formed Shango or Trinidad Orisha. In Cuba, Santeria took root. In Haiti, Vodou, more popularly known as voodoo, was created. Throughout the Caribbean, Obeah also took shape.

While all of these beliefs were born out of shared hardship, to say they are the same would be a disservice. This is especially true if one compares Obeah to Vodou. While both practices deal with spirits and seek to help others in their daily life, there are very few similarities between the two. For starters, Obeah's origins are attributed to the Ashanti people, who actually had a reputation amongst the French and Spanish for being rebellious. The British were not as timid, forcefully displacing thousands to the West Indies. Vodou, on the other hand, originated by combining the beliefs of the Dahomean, Kongo, Yoruba, and various other ethnic groups that were forced by the French to move to Haiti (McAlister, n.d.).

Besides origin differences, Obeah and Vodou also differ in how it is practiced. Obeah is primarily done by individual practitioners, and the rituals and methods are passed down from master to apprentice. In fact, like an overabundance of fantasy wizards, Obeah men or women usually inherit this power through their ancestry, meaning these master and apprentice relationships are often within the same family tree. There is a method to become an Obeah outside of such families, but the vast number of practitioners come from Obeah families.

Vodou is vastly different in these regards. Vodou has a structure that makes it more of a religion compared to its Obeah counterpart. These structures are centered around communities called *sosyete*, with the average priest being called a *manbo* or *houngan*. Priests devoted to a certain *loa*, important spirits within Vodou, are instead called an *ounsis*, though they still aid the *houngans* and *manbos* in their practice. Underneath the *ounsis* are the *petite-caye*, who serve a similar role but aren't as devoted (*Vodou and Obeah*, 2022).

The two beliefs also have different practices. Obeah has two focuses: magick and herbalism. Vodou, on the other hand, focuses primarily on group rituals meant to aid the people involved. In both cases, Obeah and Vodou conduct their practice to improve their health, romantic attractiveness, luck, and chances to evade the law. The last one may seem like a malicious act until one remembers the historical context of both practices. Obeah and Vodou were originally practiced by black people being enslaved by white people. Due to this, the rights granted to the slaves were heavily restricted, so what counts as a "crime" for a black person during that time period was far wider than that for a white person.

Obeah was actually illegal for much of its existence due to colonial pressure. White colonists, fearing that Obeah would threaten their position, passed laws to restrict the practice. This made it so Obeah practitioners had to work in secret, cementing the tradition of fixing people's problems on an individual level. Vodou found a way to circumnavigate such discrimination from affecting them, though in doing so, it brought up a new problem. In an act of disguising their faith, the early *houngans* mixed their beliefs with Catholic symbolism. Over time, this disguise became part of Vodou, though to what extent is up for debate. Some Vodou practitioners claim they are Catholics with a different name, saying the Catholic saints are the same as Vodou's *loa*. At the same time, there are practitioners that still hold the idea that Catholic symbolism is just for appearances. Like many faiths, Vodou doesn't have a head committee that determines what is and what isn't Vodou. Because of it, it is hard to gauge how much Catholicism is part of Vodou.

As said before, the Obeah focus primarily on individual practice with those seeking aid going to an Obeah man or woman to conduct a ritual for them. The Obeah practitioners also serve a protective  role, using their knowledge to help others protect themselves from malicious spirits called dupppies. This was sometimes done through the use of a fetish, an inanimate object that was carried for protection against such spirits (*Obeah and Myal*, n.d.). While the Vodou have similar goals to Obeah, their methods are different. Namely, the Vodou ask the *loa* for aid through a variety of methods. More popular examples involve drums, dancing, and being possessed by the *loa*, who in turn offer omens and blessings to their followers. Other methods include *veves*, symbols drawn out through the use of cornmeal, and voodoo dolls, which are used to attract the *loa* (Beyer, 2018a). As mentioned in a previous section, kolossoi are similar to the popular conception of a voodoo doll because voodoo doll depictions in popular media are more akin to kolossoi than actual voodoo dolls.

It should be noted that both Obeah and Vodou have variations when it comes to their practice. Vodou alone has several different distinct branches, including "Rada, Daome, Ibo, Nago, Dereal, Manding, Petwo, and Kongo" (McAlister, n.d.). Some Vodou branches practice Obeah's family structure by having familial spirits (McAlister, n.d.). Others conduct animal sacrifices in order to appease the *loa* (Beyer, 2018a). Despite these differences, Obeah, Vodou, and other beliefs that grew from a cruel period of history in the Caribbean show that even in the darkest of times, humanity will find hope and ways to empower themselves.

Powwow

Powwow, or Braucherei in Deitsch, is a type of Germanic magick mostly practiced in Pennsylvania. This form of magick was brought over by Germanic immigrants and is still practiced to some degree in the modern-day.

It should be noted that this "powwow" shouldn't be confused with the Native American powwow, which is a gathering of several indigenous communities meant to strengthen bonds between them while expressing their cultural pride. The two are not associated in any way other than the fact the two are done in North America.

Powwow is an interesting practice because similar to Vodou, it uses Christian iconography. Unlike Vodou, however, Powwow practitioners never used such symbols to hide their practice. Instead, Powwow directly connects itself with Christianity, claiming the spells are empowered by the strength of God. This creates a weird duality as Powwow has practices that one could associate with witchcraft while at the same time being fully devoted to the religion that has historically persecuted similar crafts. Yet, despite this, practitioners see themselves as no different from other Christians. In fact, in order for one to actually practice Powwow, they have to be Christian in faith.

Due to the nature of the Christian faith promoting selflessness and humility, Powwow primarily has spells focused on healing or protection. Healing spells are usually conducted through invocations that are assisted by consecrated objects and herbal remedies (Wigington, 2019b). Protection spells usually come in the form of hexes and other sacred symbols associated with Christianity. While healing and protection spells are the primary spells associated with Powwow, there is one type of Powwow magick they consider to be dark magic. According to Professor David Kriebel, *The Sixth and Seventh Books of Moses* is a volume that contains Powwow magic. Yet, unlike other books,

The Sixth and Seventh Books of Moses contain rituals that enable the summoning of spirits, a concept that most Powwow practitioners consider to be taboo (Kriebel, 2002).

Powwow literature isn't restricted to texts containing dark rituals, though. One of the most famous works was written by John George Homan in 1820 under the title *Pow-Wows: or, Long Lost Friend.* The text featured many usable rituals, remedies, and trinkets to aid Powwow doctors in their practice. More practices appear in Albertus Magnus's works, which sometimes illustrate more forms of Christian magick. Albertus Magnus himself was a German saint from the thirteenth century, spending much of his time writing books. However, these writers aren't the only teachers of Powwow. Traditionally, those who learned Powwow learned it from a practitioner of the opposite sex through the use of oral tradition and practice. Due to the multitude of healing and protection spells, most who learn the craft become "Powwow doctors," who in turn promise to help those in need and never accept money for their practice (Wigington, 2019b).

Just as times change, so does the adherence to religion. While tradition states that Powwow doctors shouldn't accept money, according to Professor Kriebel, that is no longer the case.

"'Entrepreneurial' Powwowers," as Kriebel calls them, go against tradition and expect people to pay for their services (Kriebel, 2002). While the traditional practitioners still exist, these entrepreneurial Powwowers do show that tradition does fade away in time. Still, according to Kriebel, these entrepreneurial types only really ask for payment for what he calls Type II and Type III rituals. Type I rituals are described as having no more than two ritual components, a lack of verbal components, and target a single illness or issue that is not life-threatening (Kriebel, 2002). Anything more complex or larger in terms of scope would fall into either Type II or Type III spells, though Kriebel does remark that Type II rituals have a likelihood of being conducted for free.

While God is the main power in this magick system, there is also the presence of herbal remedies. These remedies aren't simply restricted to humans nor are they only for healing. For example, in one ritual, a mixture of "wormwood, asafetida, and other herbs" are mixed with salt and "soil from your stable" (Wigington, 2019b). Once the items are mixed together, the mixture would be buried in front of a stable where livestock resides, protecting its residents from disease and theft (Wigington, 2019b). If we go by Kriebel's type categorization method, this spell would probably fit into either Type II or Type III.

The previously mentioned also shows that, while God may be the one contributing power to the Powwow doctor, his name or other holy names don't need to be invoked in order for a ritual to take effect. However, the opposite is also true. There are some spells that ask for holy aid without the use of anything material. For example, a ritual that is intended to stop bleeding involves the caster saying, "This is the day on which the injury happened. Blood, thou must stop, until the Virgin Mary brings forth another son," three times in a row (Dugan, n.d.). Rituals similar to these would fit Kriebel's category of Type I rituals, which are considered to be too simple for an entrepreneurial Powwower to charge for money.

Like many groups in the past, the Germans who originally practiced Powwow moved to America due to religious persecution back in their

home region around the 17th and 18th centuries (Wigington, 2019b). It is unclear if this religious persecution was aimed at the practice or not, as modern Germany, we know didn't exist at the time. Instead, the region was still subdivided into several kingdoms united in a confederate called the Holy Roman Empire. This makes understanding the cause of the exodus complicated due to the fact each kingdom within the confederate would have varying levels of religious tolerance. Due to this, the actual forerunners of Powwow came from several different religious backgrounds, including Lutherans, Amish, Mennonites, Anabaptists, and other Protestant groups (Wigington, 2019b). Due to these groups being primarily Protestant in nature, one could theorize that this exodus was due to that affiliation rather than their practice of Powwow, as many of the practices that would later be implemented into Powwow dated back to before the Protestant Reformation (Wigington, 2019b).

Once the Germanic community settled themselves in, not a lot of history on Powwow could be found. Since *Pow-Wows: or, Long Lost Friend* was published a century later, it seems accurate to say that no one really had a problem with the practice. However, there is one exception to that rule that brings forth a very ironic twist. According to Professor Kriebel, the modern-day "Conservative (Eastern) Mennonites" view Powwow as a "work of Satan" (Kriebel, 2002). While there is no clear indication of how old this viewpoint is, this hostility has been noted as a contributing factor to the decline of the Powwow practice. This has made finding traditional practitioners of Powwow rare, with Kriebel noting that "there is a perception within the culture area that powwowing is no longer practiced and less than half of the people I spoke with had even heard of it" (Kriebel, 2002).

Thus, Powwow lives in an ironic state, where the magick practice that devotes itself to the Christian faith is in turn denounced by Christians calling it the work of Satan. It does, unfortunately, track with history. Perhaps in time, Powwow will have a revitalization and be recognized as an interesting system of magick, or perhaps it is doomed to fade away into history like many other lost magick arts. In cither case, Powwow certainly was an interesting blend of two concepts usually opposed to one another, though the opposition was usually restricted to one party.

Satanism

While many of the other forms of magick here are very old, some are rather new. Like Wiccans, the modern Satanist is very different from previous groups that worshiped the religious figure. While there were plenty of groups that worshiped Satan, it was neither organized nor directly connected to witchcraft. The first official Satanic church was created during the 1960s through the works of writer Anton LaVey. The most famous of these works is *The Satanic Bible*, which forms the outlines of his beliefs as well as the central core of the magick practiced by modern-day Satanists.

To begin with, magick in Satanism is divided into two main categories: Lesser Magic, which is non-ritualistic in nature, and Greater Magic, which requires a ritual. Of the two, Lesser Magic is easier to pin down, as it is only divided into three additional groups: lust, nostalgia, and fear (Timon, 2016). Greater Magic on the other hand is connected to every form of "basic human emotion," which makes it more varied than Lesser Magic (Timon, 2016). Due to the emotion-centric source of Satanic magick, *The Satanic Bible* emphasizes the importance of letting one's emotions flow freely and honestly. In fact, LaVey argues that the caster needs to be honest with their own desires. If not, the spell will not work and may even backfire.

Despite popular depictions, most modern Satanists don't actually trace their power to demons, or even Satan himself. In fact, LaVey made it clear that Satan in this context is not actually a character at all, but instead a force of nature that can be drawn upon to aid a person in their day-to-day lives (Timon, 2016). This force is directly connected to human emotion, and it is through intense emotion that one can invoke the powers granted by it. This emotional state includes touching upon one's more animalistic side, as LaVey claims that acting more animalistic provides the same, if not more, power than animal sacrifices (Timon, 2016). This goes against cultural depictions of Satanists using animal or human sacrifices, both of which go against LaVey's claims that invoking magick is an internal, not external, activity.

That being said, Satanic magick isn't entirely internal. There are materials and phrases needed in order for spells to go off successfully, including symbols and incantations. These parts are just as important as one's emotional state, as the wrong words or symbols can result in negative consequences. Additionally, the caster needs to be confident during the entire casting process, including before and after the spell has been cast (Timon, 2016). If the Satanist believes the spell won't, isn't, or didn't work, then the spell will not be as strong as someone who has kept faith in themselves and the magick they invoke.

A unique factor of Satanic magick is the target of the spells. With other practices, spells could target spirits, aspects of nature, or fate itself. However, Satanic magick can only target one thing: people (Timon, 2016). This is not to say these spells are entirely malevolent or that such spells can't be used to gain other items, but Satanic magick can't target things such as negativity or weather conditions. The former could be targeted if the Satanist wishes to make a person less negative or close-minded, but a space that is perceived as negative cannot be cleansed through Satanic magick. This limited targeting means there are generally only two types of outcomes that come from spells: they either aid a person or harm a person.

Satanic spells drawing upon compassion and lust are associated with aiding a person and require both the caster and the receiver to believe in the spell for the best effect. Lust spells are meant to make intercourse more pleasurable for both parties involved, meaning they rely on the consent of everyone in order to work. Meanwhile, compassion spells are meant to generally aid a person in either health, success, or a different but similar condition. Satanists also practice spells literally called "destruction spells," which are meant to harm or destroy an individual. Ironically,

the less the target believes the destruction spell is effective, the stronger the spell is (Timon, 2016). This means that those who take Satanic magic seriously, follower or not, are less likely to be hurt by a destruction ritual compared to someone who disregards magick entirely. Additionally, people who aren't focusing, such as when they are sleeping, daydreaming, or bored, are also more susceptible to Satanic magic (Timon, 2016).

The magick LaVey describes has a philosophy that is distinctly separate from any other magick practices. Namely, LaVey believes that using words such as "good" or "evil" to describe any type of magick is ridiculous, as such ideals are based on one's relative position to magick (Timon, 2016). This means that, to a Satanist, you can't really claim that someone is doing dark magick. LaVey also addresses stage magic, which is a rarity to see when talking about magick. Rarer still is that LaVey somewhat embraces the idea that stage magic does have a bit of magick to it, though he fully recognizes that not all stage magic uses it (Timon, 2016). While not fully embraced, the presence and even discussion of stage magic being valid are unorthodox when referencing older systems of magick, which would most likely claim that stage magic is just trickery.

However, while LaVey was a bit more accepting of other concepts of magic, *The Satanic Bible* also disagrees with many other forms. Namely, LaVey rejects the notion that ancient magick is useful or has any other secrets not already present in *The Satanic Bible* (Timon, 2016). Contemporary practices are still acceptable, but practices that are long since forgotten don't have any secret powers hidden away. This is due to his retelling of history with a Satanist lens, which does have some alterations. Firstly, LaVey claims that the majority of the victims accused during the witch trials weren't witches, but instead true witches prospered in areas away from heavily populated cities and towns (Timon, 2016). Additionally, he claims that his brand of Satanists didn't fit the profile of would-be witch hunters, even claiming that some people were Satanists but just didn't know

(Timon, 2016). The biggest claim, and one that is a bit hard to swallow, is that Satanists have dominated the world and will continue to dominate the world, though they have and will brand themselves differently as time passes (Timon, 2016). He further emphasizes this by claiming a "New Satanic Age" had dawned due to the bickering on the other side of the theological argument (Timon, 2016). While this would prove ironic later on, it should be noted that Satanic magick was still a part of Satanic belief, which has declared itself a religion.

With *The Satanic Bible* published, LaVey crowned himself the first "Black Pope," a title that actually has been used several times before. However, in a very ironic turn, the Satanic church had already begun to divide itself into separate churches, some claiming to be older than LaVey's Church of Satan (History.com Editors, 2019). However, the biggest threat to Satanists wasn't internal disagreements, but external enemies. This came in the form of the 1980s Satanic Panic, a time where Christian fundamentalists claim that children were being abused during Satanic rituals and that Satanism itself encouraged its members to turn into murderers (History.com Editors, 2019). While it is true that Satanism does promote the belief that one "should feel free to pursue their own happiness," it also makes sure that their followers realize that they aren't immune to the consequences of said actions (Beyer, 2019a). On a personal level, LaVey denounced those who harmed children, did commit animal sacrifices, and even did the general illegal activity (Beyer, 2019a). These denouncements did little to ease the fears of the Christian fundamentalists, blaming multiple tragic and horrific things on Satanists with little or no proof of their involvement. However, even though the image of Satanists was dragged through the mud, those who actually became victims of this hysteria were often, similar to the witch trials of old, other Christians (History.com Editors, 2019).

The Church of Satan survived the Satanic Panic but would change soon after. LaVey died, and his death left a power gap that resulted in his partner, Blanche Barton, fighting against his children for control of the church (History.com Editors, 2019). While this changed little for the church, the true breaking point came from an author, Peter H. Gilmore, who was assigned by Barton to promote the church (History.com Editors, 2019). Gilmore claimed that the Church of Satan members were the only true Satanists, and this claim resulted in more Satanic branches forming, an event very reminiscent of the Protestant Reformation (History.com Editors, 2019).

Despite the many divisions, there are still notable Satanic churches. The Satanic Temple claims to be the new "primary religious Satanic organization in the world with congregations internationally," noting on their website that they disagree with the much older Church of Satan (*About Us*, n.d.). These differences do not stop the Satanic Temple from practicing magick, with their website providing rituals one can perform themselves. While it will most likely be a long time before they are painted in a positive light in the media, actual Satanists are just as varied as their Christian counterparts, having several different branches that can and will disagree on certain topics. However, looking into *The Satanic Bible* and LaVey's work shows a form of magick that is not only new but rather unique compared to older faiths.

Seiðr and Runes

Seiðr is a type of Norse magick or *fjölkynngi*. Seiðr is primarily seen as divination magick, though some lump other abilities onto it. Culturally speaking, Seiðr is seen as something only women are supposed to do. Why this is isn't entirely clear, though evidence suggests that part of it was due to some rituals that involved weaving and the fact it originated from the goddess Freya. Women could become professional practitioners of Seiðr, earning the title of "völva" or "seiðkona." Men could technically practice the craft to become "seiðmaðr," but being a seiðmaðr was seen as a great shame as it was seen as unmanly in Norse society. Even in a mythological sense, Odin was berated by Loki for practicing Seiðr, the trickster god claiming that Odin was acting unmanly because of it.

Though the definition of Seiðr is a bit loose; the two major uses for this magick are to either find out what fate has for a person or to shift fate for the desired outcome. How these rituals were done is up to debate as there are no clear historical records on the traditional methods or at least official ones. However, there is a consensus that claims that "seiðr was a practice in which the magician used spinning to conjure spirits" (Storesund, 2017). The "spinning" involved was not of the bodily kind but of threads. In Norse mythology, a trio of goddesses called the Norns helped form the Web of Wyrd, extending threads that craft the fates of all life. Seiðr is meant to allow the caster to peer at the crafting of the Web of Wyrd and alter it if they so choose. Thus, in order to alter the tapestry of fate, the practitioner would need to weave their alteration into the web.

Seiðr was not the only magick practiced by the Norse, however. Another form is Spá or Spae, an art similar to Seiðr in the sense that both focus on investigating the fate and how things will play out. Unlike Seiðr, however, Spá merely looks at the Web of Wyrd instead of altering it. There is also Galdr, a music-based form of magick that came in either a song or chant. However, the most commonly referenced form of magick from this group comes in the form of rune magick.

To assume that Norse runes were strictly used  for magickal purposes would be incorrect. The runes used for magick came from the actual alphabet for the Norse. Due to this, besides spells that only used runes, other forms of Norse magick, such as Spá and Galdr, also used these symbols for their rituals. Additionally, runes were used for communication and mundane tasks, so the mere presence of runes doesn't automatically indicate the application of magick. In fact, a common mistake for modern practitioners is not invoking the runes to activate their magickal properties after writing them down (Vamvoukakis, n.d.). Without invoking them, these runes just form a sentence, assuming the writer wrote the sentence correctly.

The spelling and order of the runes are very important when one is wishing to conduct a Norse rune magick. To explain it simply, how runes are arranged determines the meaning of the spell in a way similar to how the presence or absence of a comma alters an entire sentence. Just like how "Let's eat grandma" and "Let's eat, grandma" mean two different things, so too does a minor shifting of runes. A common story that is often pointed to illustrate this fact comes from the Saga of Egil Skallagrimsson.

Though the exact details are somewhat vague, the overall message and series of events are clear. One day, Egil Skallagrimsson was called to see an ill woman. Upon searching her bed, Egil found a set of runes that were making her sick. These runes weren't part of a malicious plot, however, but instead an act of an admirer who wanted to strengthen their relationship with the woman for one reason or another. Due to an incorrect arrangement of runes, this attempt at romanticizing turned deadly. Egil quickly made a new set of runes to replace the illness-causing set, resulting in the woman making a speedy recovery. This story not only details the importance of making sure you are writing the runes down in the correct order but also shows the potential harm that can be caused when they are improperly ordered.

However, merely understanding how the rune appears regularly isn't enough. There are other ways a rune can appear, and this alteration in appearance alters the meaning of the rune itself. For example, if a runc is inverted from its regular position, the original meaning becomes its opposite (Vamvoukakis, n.d.). So, an inverted Raidho, which usually means road or journey, becomes a symbol meaning to stay in one place or a state of stagnation. There are also mirrored runes, which boost the strength of the rune at the cost of a slight alteration (Vamvoukakis, n.d.). A mirrored rune appears as the name suggests, which is to make the rune appear like it would in a mirror. Think of it like making a "b" look like "d". Due to the nature of some runes, they do not have a mirror, either because it is symmetrical or because their theoretical mirror rune becomes an entirely different and preexisting rune (Vamvoukakis, n.d.). So, while all runes have an inverted rune, not all runes have a mirrored one.

The invocation of runes themselves does vary from spell to spell. As mentioned previously, rune stones can be used in a form of divination where the activation of the runes' predicting powers comes from simply posing a question. In a sense, that form of rune use aligns with the practice of Spá. However, while rune stones are one form in which runes could present themselves, it is not only one. In fact, there aren't really any historical rules about what medium runes have to be present in (Vamvoukakis, n.d.). The runes themselves do have to be legible, there is no denying that, but where these runes are placed is basically determined by the caster or carver. In fact, evidence suggests that there is some crossover between runic magick and how people regularly characterize fictional wizards. Among numerous medieval relics are staffs and wands with engraved runes on them, which were "waved at the person, who its user wished to 'catch'" the effects of the spell (*Runic Magic*, n.d.).

The Norse had a variety of magickal practices and tales associated with them, the actual art of conducting some of these rituals has been lost to time. We may never know the full extent of such magickal arts, which makes the information we have collected all the more valuable.

Thelema Magick

Thelema magick is interesting as it is another system that defines itself with the term "magick." One may assume that this is due to Thelema magick being younger than other forms discussed here. That assumption would be correct, as Thelema was first officially created in 1904 by a man named Aleister Crowley. Much of the magick described in Thelema relates back to the core of Crowley's beliefs that have become the Thelema faith. Due to this connection, it seems appropriate to examine the life of Crowley and how he eventually became the founder of a whole new belief system.

Aleister Crowley was born as Edward

Alexander Crowley in 1875 in Royal Leamington Spa, England. While he was born in a Christian household, he grew up to dislike the faith. This would later influence Thelema, but Crowley chose to express his distaste in a much more personal way during his early life. He adopted the monicor "the Beast'" and aligned himself with the number 666. However, his more famous name change didn't occur until he started going to the University of Cambridge, where he finally adopted the name Aleister Crowley.

After his time in college, he began traveling around the world in 1898. Crowley was very busy during his travels, writing a book of poetry and joining a group called the Hermetic Order of the Golden Dawn. His membership with the order was short-lived, leaving only two years later. However, the ceremonial practices of the Hermetic Order would later be incorporated into Thelema magick, as well as the yoga techniques Crowley learned during his travels (White, 2020). However, the most important event to occur during his travels was during his time in Egypt in the year 1904. During his time there, he claimed to have spoken to Horus, the Egyptian deity, who instructed him to write *The Book of Law*.

The Book of Law, or *Liber AL vel Legis*, would become the frame for the ideals expressed in the

Thelema faith. However, it was not his only book relating to Thelema. In fact, in 1929, he wrote *Magick*, a book that was aimed at explaining the true nature of magick within the Thelema system. This includes a clear definition for magick in this context as Crowley writes, "MAGICK is the Science and Art of causing Change to occur in conformity with Will" (Crowley, 1929). "Will" in this context relates back to the base belief of Thelema.

Thelema works on the principle that everyone has a "True Will." In fact, Thelema means "will" in

Greek. This "True Will" is akin to destiny, though unlike the pure concept of destiny, a person could theoretically never reach their True Will. In order to even understand if one is on the right path to discover their True Will, a person needs to find their unique traits and qualities to discover their "True Self" (Beyer, 2019b). Not discovering one's True Self isn't entirely bad, as people could accidentally follow their True Will without realizing it. However, according to Crowley, misery and a lack of productivity is caused by a person going against their True Will, such as "a boy's instinct may tell him to go to sea, while his parents insist on his becoming a doctor. In such a case, he will be both unsuccessful and unhappy in medicine" (Crowley, 1929). Since misery is caused by going against one's True Will, following one's True Will results in happiness and the best results from a person's abilities.

Now, this does raise a concern. Supposedly, what if a True Will of one contradicts the True Will of another? According to Crowley, "Every man has a right to fulfill his own will without being afraid that it may interfere with that of others; for if he is in his proper place, it is the fault of others if they interfere with him" (Crowley, 1929). While this quote isn't directly related to that question, it does help answer it if we looked beyond the individual. If a group of people follow Crowley's teachings and commit to their True Will, according to this statement, no one within that group should be "interfering" with other members. If there is, then it was that individual's choice to cause harm or inconvenience to another person. This means that, while True Wills may be different from person to person, the accomplishment of one's True Will shouldn't block another person from achieving their True Will.

One might rightfully ask what any of this has to do with Thelema magick. The simple answer is that Thelema magick is different from other forms of magick when it comes to purpose. When observing the other kinds, one can get a general theme: magick is used to help a person gain something through the use of ritual. Sometimes these magick systems have no ties with destiny, and other times, they directly influence the flow of destiny. Magick in Thelema is solely used to help achieve one's destiny, or in this case, True Will. This minor difference means a person needs to be very self-aware about their wants and desires, as going against one's True Will with magick results in the same consequence as going against one's True Will in every other situation: misery and a lack of productivity.

There are other things that separate Thelema magick from other types. Firstly, Crowley claims that "Every intentional act is a Magical Act" (Crowley, 1929). While there are certain rituals in Thelema magick, akin to Kotodama with their ever-present power of certain words, every action intentionally conducted is considered to hold magick power for followers of Thelema. This concept doesn't stray too far from the definition Crowley used to explain Thelema magick where it is used to align the person and world closer to one's True Will. Since every action has consequences, using actions to get closer to one's Will would make such actions magickal in nature.

However, seeing how one can conduct actions that can result in going against one's True Will, it can be assumed that magick conducted can both help and harm the caster in this context.

Thelema magick, while still being relatively new in terms of magick systems, does inherit a trait most commonly found in older forms of magick and religion. Thelema magick incorporates science into its overall structure, with text supporting an alchemic flair to Crowley's views on the subject. Crowley does admit that "we cannot cause eclipses, for instance, or transform lead into the tin, or create men from mushrooms," though he does say that "it is theoretically possible to cause in any object any change of which that object is capable by nature" (Crowley, 1929). The only thing preventing us from doing the things he admits we cannot do is, according to him, the knowledge and power we currently lack.

As noted previously, two major influences on magick rituals in the Thelema faith are rituals conducted by the Hermetic Order of the Golden Dawn and yoga practices. These rituals may not be totally separate from everyday actions in terms of purpose, but they are designed to better strengthen a person's perception of their personal True Will. However, Crowley did experiment with a type of magick that could be seen as controversial by several.

In 1912, Crowley became head of the Ordo Templi Orientis (OTO), a fraternity overseen by a German socialist by the name of Theodor Reuss (White, 2020). The fraternity sought to unify all Masonic and Hermetic systems into one connected system. This includes a type of magic that Crowley began experimenting with in the year 1914: sexual magick (White, 2020). As sexual magick is a very complex topic that requires a lot of nuances, this book will not be going into that subject matter. The necessity of mentioning it in the first place is to show that Crowley's life was not free of controversy. In fact, one could say it was plagued by it.

In 1905, while traveling up Kanchenjunga, one of the largest mountains in the world, Crowley's group encountered an avalanche. Some claim that Crowley ignored the cries of his fellow expedition members as they struggled against the cold and snow (The Editors of Encyclopaedia Britannica, 2021). Additionally, in 1923, a young man died in Sicily after supposedly doing Thelemic rituals. This event would later result in Crowley being forced out of Italy, with the OTO branch in the region slowly drifting away into obscurity (White, 2020). However, OTO is still around today and is considered the largest Thelemic organization, consisting of about 4,000 members (White, 2020).

While Crowley's life could be seen as morally gray, the system of magick he created is unique in several aspects. Additionally, researchers have contributed great power to Crowley's work and philosophy. Some claim that Crowley helped jump-start many of the newer magick faiths that would develop, while others examine how Crowley's individualistic philosophy influenced society. If you wish to explore and maybe even practice Thelema magick, remember that even though Thelema magick is focused on an individual's unique True Will, your True Will shouldn't prevent people from engaging with their own True Will.

Wuism

Also referred to as Chinese shamanism, Wuism is not one unified set of spells or rituals, but instead an umbrella term to refer to several similar forms of magick conducted by the several ethnic groups that are now part of present-day China. While still practiced today to some extent, Wuism is unique due to its history. Like witchcraft in Europe, practitioners of Wuism were discriminated against, but at the same time, some practitioners were venerated. This paradoxical nature has a

direct relationship with Chinese centralization.

In the very beginning of Wuism, both males and females were considered able to conduct the practice. While certain documents differentiate the practitioners by sex, calling men practitioners *xi* or shamans and women as *wu* or shamanesses, it is more common that practitioners were simply referred to as *wu*. Like many fictional depictions of magic, not everyone can become a *wu*. According to archaeologist Tong Enzheng, "the ancient *wu* was unusual from birth. Whether they were possessed by supernatural beings or embarked on a spiritual journey, *wu* needed to be preternaturally sensitive in their emotions" (Enzheng, 2002). Despite this unusualness, the *wu* wasn't discriminated against at this time. They were instead seen as an important member of their family and their community, using their power to predict fortunes and misfortunes that members of their village would encounter (Enzheng, 2002). A thing to note was that this ability wasn't seen as a full occupation, simply an additional responsibility a *wu* had in order to support their community.

Then China began to centralize. The *wu*'s unique position allowed them to obtain higher status becoming part of the elite class (Enzheng, 2002). This rise also gave rise to emperors claiming to be *wu*. Amongst these was the Yellow Emperor who claimed to have the ability to speak to spirits and Emperor Shun who was said to have perfect navigational abilities (Enzheng, 2002). Along with the classification's increased prestige, the roles and responsibilities of the *wu* changed. Alongside their previous responsibilities as *wu*, the practitioners became judges, writers, calendric and astrological observers, doctors, and record keepers (Enzheng, 2002).

Despite this rise in power, *wu*'s position wasn't always a kind one. During the rule of Tang of the Shang Dynasty, a story claims that Tang himself suffered and prayed for forgiveness during a drought that devastated the land. The gods, feeling pity, sent down hard rain that countered the devastation caused by the drought. This act inspired similar rituals where *wu* would be bound, nude, and exposed to the elements in order to invoke divine pity and rain (Enzheng, 2002). Alongside potentially deadly rituals, the political power of *wu* began to dissipate, with the earliest period of this decline happening during the Western Zhou dynasty, which started around 1050 B.C. (Enzheng, 2002). However, even with decreased power, *wu* were still used for their divination abilities, though the divinations that were being asked for now focused more on the state instead of a single community or family.

Despite many *wu* being in higher positions of power, there were still records of *wu* on a local level that conduct much of the same rituals conducted by their earlier incarnations. However, even though local *wu* was conducting historical practices that many were fine with for decades, they were discriminated against by the Chinese government in this new age. This came from a differentiation in the practices conducted between the elite, sanctioned *wu,* and the local *wu.* Those *wu* in positions of authority claimed to have their power tied to divine deities and spirits. In contrast, the local *wu* still cited their visions as coming from the aid of spirits that weren't technically gods or goddesses. This division in faith created a divide between the two types of *wu,* resulting in discrimination that disproportionately harmed those who stuck with the old faith. Thus, practitioners of Wuism were both discriminated against and venerated.

Beyond history, Wuism is different from much of the magick discussed in this book. While rituals make up the bulk of the practice, these rituals are different as they are primarily conducted

through music and dance. The exact procedure of the spell depended on the practitioner's background and placement in society as local *wu* usually conducted the dance by themselves, unlike their more structured counterparts in the government who practiced in groups. However, one unifying factor that seems present in the majority of rituals were drums. Archaeologist Enzheng noted that in many recorded rituals, "the drum was the most significant instrument," even during wartime. This was because, even before a battle, drums "were still associated with magical dancing" and were used "to boost the fighting spirit of one's own side and to threaten the enemy" (Enzheng, 2002). The combination of music and dance in order to cast spells is an uncommon concept, even in fictional stories where they use the former without the latter.

In addition to these practices, a subgroup of *wu* emerged called the *fangshi*, which can translate to "recipe master." While they were still considered *wu*, the *fangshi* were strictly part of the elites who worked for the Chinese government. While they conducted the duty excepted by every *wu* practitioner of their time, they are most famous for their potion-making. Specifically, they are famous for their research into an elixir of immortality. They were more than that, though, being what many would consider being scientists nowadays, with them conducting experiments to see what happens when compounds are mixed together.

Wuism today is still a bit of a touchy subject for China. During the development of the First Republic of China, certain branches of Wuism were forbidden and the elite *wu* practitioners lost their post (Naef-Tahvanainen, 2014). However, as recently as 2014, this perspective has begun to change alongside China's efforts to reintroduce and praise China's historical culture, though the practice does have some new governmental influence (Naef-Tahvanainen, 2014). Even if it gets rejected again in the future, Wuism will most likely endure as it had for centuries.

Chaos Magic

Chaos magic is not an actual system of magick, and yet, at the same time, it is. If one recalls all the way back in Chapter 1, eclectic witches are a type of witch that incorporates several practices into a singular, personal practice. Chaos magic works the same way with one minor difference: there is no personal practice. Sure, someone practicing Chaos magic can use the same rituals over and over again, but they don't *have* to. Chaos magic focuses on the here and now. Any rituals conducted by a Chaos magician are done because the magician themselves think it will work for a specific time and place. If the next day they wish to conduct another spell in order to get the same effect, the Chaos magic practitioner can reject the old spell and conduct a new one. The second spell doesn't invalidate the first, for, at both times, the practitioner believes the spells will work.

"How does this make any sense?" one could ask themselves. It is a very valid question. All the previous magick systems, even if they have divergences between groups who claim the same practice, have some level of consistency. While Chaos magicians may disagree on the exact specifics of the source of magick in this context,

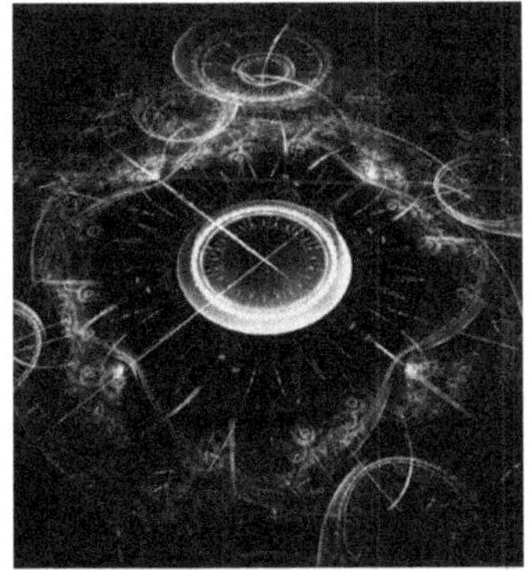

the general idea is that magick is something invoked by the person, not the actions directly. Chaos magicians see rituals as a method to get into the proper state of mind that enables them to perform magick, but the ritual itself is overall meaningless. The caster's intentions have more power than the performance they conduct.

Compared to the other forms of magick, Chaos magic is an outlier when it comes to freedom of practice as there is no concrete way to describe the practice. That being said, while the practice itself is chaotic, the history behind it is not. While it would be appropriate for Chaos magic to be thought up by several individuals all at the same time, in an ironic twist, most people associated the formation of Chaos magic with one writer: Austin Osman Spare.

Austin Osman Spare was born in December 1886 in London, England. At an early age, Spare had a talent for art, a talent of his that he used to his fullest. In 1904, despite being only in his teens, his work was accepted into the Royal College of Arts summer exhibition, solidifying his career as an artist for a brief period of time, but time passed and his favor with critics slowly died out. It was around this time that Spare began to investigate magick practices. This investigation eventually led Austin Spare to meet a key occultist figure of the time: Aleister Crowley.

At first, Spare and Crowley were friendly toward one another. However, as Spare looked further into the structured faith organized by Crowley, the more hostile the two became towards each other. Spare began to outwardly criticize the ceremonial practices that "prevented the practitioner from discovering his/her own power" (*Chaos Magick*, 2022). Desiring to make an alternative, Spare created a sigil form of magick that was designed to be easier than Crowley's Thelemic rituals. In truth, while Spare did create the base of what would eventually be Chaos magic, Spare never actually called what he did "chaos magic," nor was his sigil magick a prototype for said practice (Beyer, 2018b). However, his criticisms would eventually inspire other writers to challenge ceremonial practices that would lead to the formation of Chaos magic.

Ray Sherwin and Peter J. Carroll are two such writers. The two published works around the same time, making it hard to determine who was the more influential of the two. Sherwin mostly wrote works promoting Chaos Magic, including *The Book of Results* in 1983 and *The Theatre of Magick* in 1989 (*Chaos Magick*, 2022). In contrast, Carroll helped create several Chaos magician covens during the 1970s and 1980s (Beyer, 2018b). Carroll did write after Sherwin's works were published, with *Psychonaut* being one where Carroll covers the theory and practice of Chaos magic (*Chaos Magick*, 2022). While one could argue over who was the larger contributor to the practice, no one can deny that the two at least contributed to the spread and continuation of Chaos magic practices.

The most fascinating aspect of Chaos magic is the fact that everything in this book could theoretically be used for this system of magick. While the rituals themselves are meaningless to a Chaos magician, the act of conducting them enables their magick to prosper. While they might not adopt the significance of earlier chapters, they may mimic the motions in order to conduct their own spells. The same couldn't be said for other casters in this text, as some practices conducted by one type conflict or avoid practices done by another group. In an ironic sense, Chaos magicians might be one of the most unifying of all; unified in a practice of inconsistency.

CONCLUSION

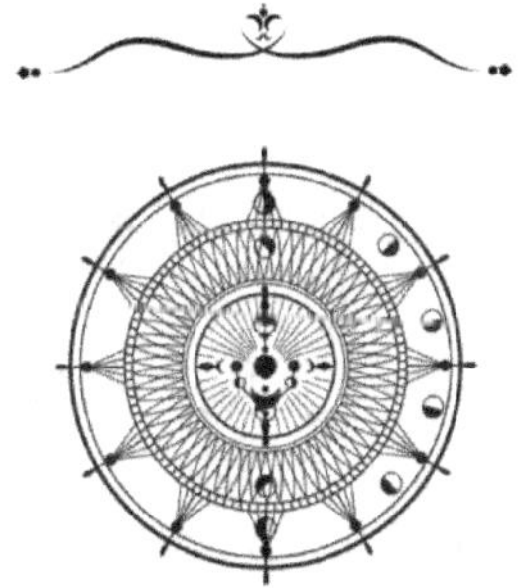

Media likes to portray magic as this earth-shattering thing that could rip the world apart if placed into the hands of evil people. Real magick is neither that grandiose nor that powerful. However, throughout the ages, people around the world have found it reliable in one form or another. From the witches, both modern and old, who use magick to cast spells, to the astrologists and numerologists who examine the world through observations, and to the druids and other practitioners who tap into ancient practices, magick has been used to make predictions and to alter the world in much more subtle ways.

This book went over the complex history many of these systems have as well as some of the beliefs around them. Materials used for spells were analyzed to see what their purpose is and how one may apply them to one's own rituals. This guide went over how to prepare for a spell and how to conduct it, including how one can make their own magic circle. This book helped show a process about how one can make their very own spells if they so choose. Finally, this book explored alternative forms of magick that have their own systems, many connected to a complex philosophy and history that separates them from their peers.

To those young spellcasters wishing to conduct their first rituals, congratulations. This is by no means a fully detailed book going over everything about spells, but this should be more than enough to get you started on your first spells. Just remember that spells aren't going to fix all your problems. They can help alleviate some of the work, but you still have to put in the effort in your day-to-day life. The less a spell has to change, the more likely it will succeed.

To the more skeptical among you, your misgivings on accepting the validity of magick are perfectly fine. This book was by no means an argument about the truthfulness of the practice, merely a guide to it. Hopefully, you've learned something from this text. Perhaps you discovered the truly complex nature of witchcraft. Perhaps you found the history surrounding the different magick practitioners interesting and wish to learn more about a group's history. Maybe this book has piqued your interest in exploring other topics related to magick, even if you don't believe in it. Whatever it is, I hope you find some joy in reading this book. Who knows? Perhaps you might try making a spell one day.

CURSE BE GONE

INTRODUCTION

A witch ought never to be frightened in the darkest forest because she should be sure in her soul that the most terrifying thing in the forest was her. – Terry Pratchett

Us witches know that magick is real and that it is powerful. Sure, we can't launch fireballs out of our hands or rustle up a big win on the lottery—after all, it's magick not miracles— but we know, deep in the  place within our guts where our intuition lies, that magick can achieve many things that others wouldn't dare think possible. Whether it's bringing greater prosperity into your life or helping you find that special someone, magick can be used for all sorts of purposes to great effect.

Note the use of the alternative spelling "magick" here. This is to distinguish the practices of true witchcraft and sorcery from the sort of stage magic a magician may perform at a child's party (Kraig, 2010). We're not pulling rabbits out of a hat, here; we are making material change in the universe based on our intentions, actions, and energies.

Perhaps, you are already familiar with magick. In that case, the book in your hands will act as an excellent supplement to your preexisting magickal library, helping you to add to your current repertoire. But you may, instead, be someone who is only just starting out, interested in magick but unsure what it's about or where to begin. It makes sense, then, to add a brief introduction to the practices of magick and witchcraft before I continue with why magickal self-defense is important. Indeed, many advanced witches agree that defensive magick is the best place for newbie witches to start, so you've come to the right place.

What Is Magick?

Magick, like religion, has likely existed since time immemorial. While religion focuses on the actions of deities and other cosmic beings—often petitioning them for aid or trying to ascend to be closer to them—magick instead draws attention to the self and what we can do using our own power. The two are often intertwined to create a cohesive system of belief that involves both worship and spell-craft. This can be seen throughout history, such as with the Ancient Greeks, as well as in the modern day, in neopagan religions such as Wicca and Druidism

(Fowler, 1995).

Indeed, so common is this intermingling of magick and religion into Wicca in particular that many believe all witches are Wiccan. This, however, is not the case. One can follow any religion—even Christianity—or none at all and still be a witch because of the already-stated distinction between the two spiritual systems. So, while pretty much all Wiccans are witches, not all witches are Wiccan.

To better understand magick, it makes sense to come to a common definition. There is an often repeated quote from infamous occultist Aleister Crowley—who was not without his problems—that states that magick is the "Science and Art that provokes Change in conformity with the Will" (What is magic? Aleister Crowley explains, 2020). The actual practice of magick involves more than intention, however.

Magick presupposes the existence of typically unseen forces and energies that can still, with practice, be perceived and manipulated. These energies run through all things, from the universe as a whole down to a grain of sand. We each contain within us part of the divine spark of creation, showing the symbiotic way we exist with the world and creatures that surround us. We all also have an energy that is specific to the type of being we are, as well as who we are as individuals, too. This means that while each lavender plant is an individual, it will still carry the same sort of traits that other plants like it do—something that we'll see when we come to correspondences in Chapter 3.

The universe itself is alive with all these forces, working to its own rhythm, but with practice, we can tap into this and manipulate the flows of energy to do our bidding. The notion that everything contains some form of energy or consciousness—no matter how different that looks from our own—is called "animism." While this might take a while to get your head around if you've been raised in a Christian culture, it is actually a common belief in non-Western spiritualities and religions.

Additionally, the belief in the divinity of the universe itself is "pantheism." Many witches recognize divinity and the universe to be one and the same thing, although some perceive the divine to extend beyond even this, existing outside the boundaries of space and time. This belief system is called "panentheism." Those are a lot of words that might take a while to get used to, but knowing the basics of these different belief systems allows you to come to your own conclusion about spiritual matters and how these then go on to intersect with the practice of witchcraft and magick. This is important because it is by reaching out with our own energy and interacting with those of others that we achieve our magickal aims. They can be collaborated with and manipulated in such a way that the change reverberates throughout the cosmos, causing our desired effect.

As a simple example, we may pour our intentions into a bay leaf with a wish written on it, and then burn it over a candle to release that intention and energy into the world. Before we know it, we've passed the test we needed to take, have secured a new job, or landed ourselves a hot date at the weekend. All of this is possible with magick and more.

Debunking Myths About Magick

Unfortunately, there are a number of myths and misconceptions out there about magick and witchcraft which are unhelpful to hold when learning more about these sacred practices. I've already debunked two of these: the idea that magick doesn't really exist and that all witches are Wiccan. As I have shown, both of these beliefs are false, borne out of ignorance of the occult—understandable, really, when you consider that the word "occult" can be defined as "hidden from view" and "not easily apprehended or understood (Merriam-Webster, n.d.-a). Most of us carry at least one or two misconceptions about this because we simply do not know any better. It's just how we were brought up in a culture that sees the occult as mere superstition or something to be mocked.

To help dismantle these ideas which blinker us from the realities of magick, I'll now list a few more of these myths and debunk them so that you have a clear understanding of what is and is not true. This is vital because believing any of these falsities will only be a hindrance to learning what is to come. It's important, then, to get a grip on these basics before you continue on your path.

Magick Is Evil

There is often talk about "white magick" and "black magick," and many people think that only the latter exists. In this dualistic framework, white magick is seen as that which is beneficial—

encouraging healing, bringing prosperity, increasing the chances of finding love, and so on. Black magick, on the other hand, is that which is baneful, such as cursing enemies, forcing someone to fall in love with someone else, or binding people's actions and free will.

However, instead of me saying that black magick is not "real magick," or that it is forbidden, I am going to follow a different track by saying this: Magick is a tool. Just like a knife can be used for cutting veggies or stabbing someone, magick can be used for nice or nasty purposes. In this respect, then, it is amoral, meaning it lacks a moral component whatsoever. It is, instead, the will of the practitioner that can be said to be good or bad.

There is also the quandary of what is good or bad, in the first place. Let's take a look at two examples: Firstly, if someone were to cast a spell for them to get a job, but it then prevented someone who was living in poverty from gaining employment, can that not be said to be harmful magic? Secondly, if a witch binds a bully who then cannot abuse whoever it is they are picking on, can that not be said to be beneficial magic? Morality isn't as simple as the dualism between black and white tells us. Instead, there is a continuum that is every shade of gray imaginable. This is the real reason why saying "magick is evil" or "all magick is black magick" is unhelpful.

Moreover, there are other issues with this characterization of magick as "white = good, black = evil." In popular culture, black magick is usually associated with African diasporic religions such as Hoodoo and Haitian Vodou, both of which are often mistakenly called "voodoo" (Murphy, 1990; Newman, 2023). On the other hand, depictions of white witches practicing "good" magick in films and television shows such as Sabrina the Teenage Witch, Buffy the Vampire Slayer, and others, all depict the kind caster as a white person—usually a pretty young woman but sometimes a maternal older lady. This shows that it is usually the magick practitioner that is considered "Other," in turn causing the magick itself to be racialized, demonized as "black magick," and therefore thought of as evil. We should, then, be considerate of the thorny issue of implicit racial bias when using these terms. Often, it is better to be specific about what you mean rather than reverting to the black/white dichotomy, such as by saying "baneful magick" to refer to that which aims to harm.

Only Women Can Be Witches

A witch is simply someone of any gender who practices witchcraft, even if pop culture often depicts only women, as I covered above. There is a belief that it was only women, too, who were burned at the stake during the witch hunts. In fact, around 10–15% of people who were burned—or hanged, as was more often the case—after being accused of witchcraft were male (Witchcraft: Eight myths and misconceptions, n.d.). This means that we should not gatekeep the term from people who identify with it because we all have a collective history tied to the persecution of individuals, usually living on the margins of society, as witches.

Sometimes, this belief comes from the erroneous claim that (cisgender) women are more magickally inclined than those assigned male at birth. Frankly, this is hogwash: There is nothing about a uterus or other reproductive organs that provide someone with more magickal ability than those without them. This is simply gatekeeping the terminology from people based on prejudice against them. While the intent to lift up women comes from a good place, doing so in this way is spreading misinformation and becomes exclusionary of anyone not in the "in-group." We should avoid these myths at all costs and instead work towards a witchcraft that is inclusive of all who are interested in it.

You Have to Be Initiated or Born Into Being a Witch

Some people are fortunate enough to be born to a family of witches. Some people, too, seek out traditions that require initiation in order to join them, such as Gardnerian Wicca. However, just because this is sometimes the case doesn't mean it always is.

While it may give you a head start in training to be a witch if one or both of your parents are also witches—particularly because folk magick traditions contain a lot of oral history that is passed down through the generations—it is not essential to have "witch blood," as some call it. Being born into a family of witches does not make your magick naturally stronger than those who have come to find the practice themselves. It just means you're more likely to have learned about it at a younger age.

As well as this, back in 1989, Scott Cunningham published his famous Wicca: A Guide for the Solitary Practitioner, which put forward a form of Wicca that could be practiced by the individual without initiation into a coven. While some people do go on to choose to make their own self-initiation ritual if they are a solitary practitioner, this is not required, either. To be a witch, one must simply practice witchcraft, and there are plenty of practices outside of Wicca, such as Traditional Witchcraft, which require no formal initiation into the craft unless the witch decides to create one for themselves.

However, it should be said that some

practices are closed. This means that certain traditions shut out outsiders, usually because colonialism put these practices at risk of appropriation, theft, or forced assimilation into the dominant culture. For instance, Native American spirituality is closed to those who are not Indigenous, and some practices may even be closed to those not within a certain tribe. This is because this spirituality came under threat during colonialism, and certain practices were stolen and bastardized while the people they originated from were punished for carrying out their own religious beliefs. In order to protect the rich heritage and legacy of Indigenous cultures, these practices have essentially had their doors closed to strangers and can only be shared in special circumstances when the tribe in question gives an invitation to outsiders. It is important to honor this desire for privacy and respect, and that means not cherrypicking from these practices. Other closed practices include Hoodoo, Haitian Vodou, and Kabbalah.

This idea of practices being closed differs from malicious gatekeeping because it is an effort to protect marginalized cultures from theft and appropriation, as well as acknowledging that certain practices require certain knowledge that could only be obtained from living within a specific culture your whole life. However, there are fortunately plenty of open practices from across the world that can be engaged with to create your own spiritual system, such as Wicca, Traditional Witchcraft, and various European folk magicks and ancient religions. It is for this reason that it is unnecessary to cause upset by delving into practices closed to you.

You Have to Be Psychic to Be a Witch

While it certainly helps to be in touch with psychism if one is to practice witchcraft, this is by no means essential. However, it should be said that, as Mat Auryn (2020a) states in his book Psychic Witch, everyone has latent psychic powers. We are conditioned out of having these, typically at some point in childhood, because of societal norms and denials of the magick that surrounds us. How many children  come across as spooky, talking to things that other people can't see or having imaginary friends who seem a little bit too real? While, of course, not all instances of this are because children are communicating with spirits—indeed, most will be the product of children's wonderfully overactive imaginations—there are occasionally times when the behavior of a child can only be explained as supernatural. Unfortunately, though, we train our children to ignore these experiences, and over time, they are shut off from their "clair senses." The psychic senses that are shut off from most of us are as follows (Auryn, 2020a):

- **Clairvoyance:** The ability to see things that others can't, such as spirits.
- **Clairaudience:** The ability to hear things that others can't.
- **Clairgustance:** The same as above, except for taste.
- **Clairtangency:** The same as above, except for touch and physical sensations upon the body.
- **Clairalience:** The same as above, except for smell.
- **Clairempathy:** The ability to detect and feel the emotions of others.
- **Clairsentience:** The feeling of physical sensations within the body without a mundane explanation.
- **Claircognizance:** Knowing information that you could not otherwise

know.

These latent powers can be trained and tapped into with some effort.

Additionally, anyone can learn to use tools to practice divination, which is the uncovering of secret information and delving into what the future may hold should all things stay on the same trajectory—for we cannot deny the uncanny ability of free will to throw a spanner in the works! There are plenty of books on the market to help you pick up the basics of Tarot cards, for instance—indeed, I even wrote one myself (Visconti, 2019).

A word of caution, however: Usually, the hearing or seeing of things that others cannot perceive can have mundane explanations. Carbon monoxide poisoning, for example, does very strange things to the brain. On top of this, estimates place the incidence rate of psychosis in the American population anywhere between 1.5% and 5%(Calabrese and Al Kahlili, 2023). Psychosis is the existence of hallucinations and delusions—unusual thought patterns that are fervently believed—usually together but not always. This means that any new experiences that seem unexplainable should, first of all, be investigated for mundane causes such as these illnesses and others.

To be responsible witches, we must distinguish between the magickal and the mundane often, as otherwise, we can easily fall down rabbit holes that result in very tricky mental situations. While psychism and magick are both very much real, we should still be skeptical to a degree and practice discernment before jumping to the conclusion that something is an otherworldly or spiritual occurrence. Distinguishing between natural and magickal causes is covered further in Chapter 2.

The Importance of Magickal Self-Defense

Magick can be used for many a good thing. However, it's not always so rosy. Some magickal practitioners will have no qualms in directing the universe to wreak havoc against others, such as their rivals or those that they feel have "wronged" them in some way—whether or not this is actually the case is all rather academic when you have a curse hurtling towards you.

Sometimes, too, our magick acts like a magnet, drawing the attention of entities we'd rather not tangle with. In his book Psychic Witch, Mat Auryn (2020a) talks about being pestered by spirits constantly, only to realize he is the only witch within his area, and so, the magick he is practicing is drawing the attention of inquisitive spirits to his home like moths to a flame. While most of these spirits are harmless and simply curious about what's going on, you may not want them there at all, or you may, in rare instances, attract the attention of one whom no one would want around. Spirits are like people, after all, and while most are happy to go about their own lives, some like to be bothersome.

It is for these reasons that many of us suggest beginner witches start their practice by learning protection magick, as I said above. To this, we can also add reversals and banishings as it is better to be able to do something before an issue potentially springs up on you, perhaps catching you unawares.

Don't fear, though: While it is always best to keep yourself protected in a variety of ways at all times, it is unlikely that you will come under any of these attacks. However, because they can cause many deleterious effects if they are made, it is good to make sure your shields are up to protect you in the event of them happening. Better to be safe than sorry, as the old saying goes, and we witches know the powers contained in such old adages.

This book, then, is a one-stop source for creating your own psychic and magickal arsenal and warding against harm created by irresponsible practitioners or spirits with a malevolent (or simply annoying) agenda. Having been a practicing witch myself for many years now—indeed, I've authored a lot of books on the matter—I am in the position to pass on the wisdom that I have learned during my own magickal journey. This book represents the best of my knowledge about self-defensive magick. Read on, and become prepared for anything to come your way.

CHAPTER 1
UNDERSTANDING MAGICK FOR SELF-DEFENSE

Great results can be achieved with small forces. – Sun Tzu

It is wise to first gain an understanding of what magickal self-defense looks like before trying to dive headfirst into spells. Having a sound knowledge of the practices of magickal self-defenses—including where they come from and their historical manifestations—will allow you to plot out what your own arsenal needs to include.

It is also important to talk about our responsibilities as magickal practitioners and our codes of ethics. As I have already said, magick itself is a tool—an amoral apparatus that you control to enact your will. Ethics applies to these intentions as well as the wider ramifications of a spell's outcome. It is good practice to think about these ethical considerations before practicing magic, and so, I will deal with them in this chapter, too.

The Basics of Self-Defensive Magick

There are a number of different types of spells that make up self-defensive magick. Some are proactive, meaning you do them to prevent harm coming your way or to catch it before it penetrates into you. Others are reactive steps you would take should you come under psychic or magickal attack. In this latter category, these can be broken down further into the reversal of hexes—which sometimes also includes a return-to-sender spell—and the banishing of negative energies and malevolent spirits.

Protective Magick

Spells for protection, sometimes called "apotropaic magick" in more academic texts, are frequently referred to as "wards." Looking at the definition for this word, Merriam-Webster (n.d.-c) describes a ward as "the action or process of guarding." This is an appropriate definition for this type of magick, too. Wards are essentially a way of guarding yourself and what's yours from outside interference. They are the metaphorical lock on your door that keeps out the things you don't want coming in.

Many practitioners talk about "layered" wards. This means having multiple wards at once aimed at different things and protecting you in different ways. For example, many witches ward themselves personally from negative influence using an amulet that they wear on their person. They may then hang an iron horseshoe above their front door to prevent evil from entering the house—as well as to encourage luck, for spells can be about more than one thing at once—as is an old folk charm from England (King, 2016). Finally, they may also craft a "witch bottle," originally designed to protect against witchcraft but now commonly used as an aggressive means of protection which "bites back" against any untoward influences attempting to make their way into a property (Meier, 2019). We will cover witch bottles more below, but suffice to say, these examples show the many ways different wards can be used for the protection of both persons and property at the same time.

Additionally, the more wards you have, the harder it is for negativity or harm to break through. It's like locks, again: Only one on the door means that, with force, someone or something may be able to break through, but several layered up makes it a much more formidable target.

Reversal Magick: Hex-Breaking and Return-to-Sender

Reversal magick is reactive. This means you carry it out when you sense or divine that you have been affected by a hex, curse, or psychic attack. I'll cover the differences between these in the next chapter, as well as how to figure out whether or not you are under the effect of these.

There are two ways that you may go about doing a reversal: You may choose to break the spell to release its influence on you. The alternative is to go harder and perform a return-to-sender. This essentially takes the curse and reverts it back to whence it came.

There is much debate over the ethics of this in the witchcraft community as it can be seen as a form of baneful magic, in the same way that the aggressive witch bottle above may also be seen—due to the fact it attacks that which tries to enter. It is up to you to decide, given the circumstances, whether or not you will simply dismantle an attack against you or return it to whoever sent it. However, it is worth knowing more about both of these methods, and so, each will be covered in depth in Chapter 6.

Banishing

Sometimes, entities you don't want in your space will come in, usually to be nosey and see what's going on. Magick can, but won't always, draw the attention of curious spirits as I detailed in the previous chapter. If you'd rather have no truck with them, you can politely but firmly tell them to leave. Most will do so. A thorough cleanse of your space after this—we'll get to what cleansing is in Chapter 4—is enough to revert the energy of your home back to normal.

However, there are rarer circumstances in which more persistent visitors, who may or may not be causing trouble, come to your space. In these instances, you need to be a bit more heavy-handed. A banishing is in order when you cannot get an entity to leave your space with polite words and a nudge out the door with a cleanse followed by a more stern command to go. A banishing is essentially a spell performed to kick them out of the space, and it is often then followed up by renewing wards or creating new ones to prevent them from coming back.

Even if you have zero interest in spirit work, it is best to only banish when absolutely necessary. You wouldn't throw rocks at the salesperson on your doorstep: Telling them you're not interested is enough to get rid of them. But when things start to go awry and the interfering being won't leave, it is appropriate to bring out the big guns, as it were.

While it is rare indeed to need to banish an entity, it does unfortunately happen sometimes. That's why it's best to be prepared with knowledge in advance so that you're not scrambling around trying to create a ritual when one is sorely needed. Knowledge and planning is a key part of being a witch, and so, in Chapter 6, I'll go through the basics of banishing.

The History and Cultural Significance of Self-Defensive Magick

Self-defensive spells and charms have been around as long as magick has—a very long time, indeed. To get a better idea of what this can involve, it's worth having a look at history to see how people have protected themselves over the millennia. I'll start where it makes the most sense, with the Ancient World, before looking at Medieval magick, too. Finally, we'll take a look at examples of some of the most common forms of self-defensive magick, as well as at the concept of the evil eye, which is commonly spoken about in the folk magick traditions of Europe and pops up on social media as a trending topic periodically.

The Ancient World

The cultures of antiquity are not a monolith. They do have protective magick in common in the vaguest sense, but the symbolism and methods used vary. I'll outline just a few examples below so that you have a wider knowledge base than if I delved more deeply into just one area. This will allow you to compare and contrast the types of magick being used, which will help you when it comes to crafting your own spells.

The Ancient Greeks

The Ancient Greeks had many different forms of protective symbols. One of these was the decapitated head of Medusa—the gorgon slain by Perseus—whose head, in mythology, was placed upon Athena's shield, the Aegis. Another symbol was the disembodied eye, which harkens to the use of the famous blue nazar—sometimes known as a "mati"—which is used for protection against the evil eye (covered more below) in the present day (Habib, 2017; Hargitai, 2018; Volandes, 2020).

A form of reactive magick can be seen in their so-called "curse tablets," known as defixiones in Latin and katadesmoi in Ancient Greek. These were essentially spells that bound the actions of an enemy. While these tablets were commonly used to silence or incapacitate rivals, or to tie a desired lover to one's self, some are classed as spells of justice. These were typically encouragements for thieves to return stolen objects by punishing them in the meantime, usually through the petitioning of a deity to dole out penalties on the magickal practitioner's behalf. Magick practitioners put much effort into showing the deity in question the righteousness of their cause and how their actions were proportionate to the harm done to them. These tablets were made by carving a pliable material (usually lead), rolling it up, and piercing it with a nail. There is the potential, however, that other materials were used and they have been lost to time due to decay, such as papyrus. The rolled-up tablet was then placed within an appropriately magickal place, such as a grave or a temple to the god petitioned (Versnel, 1991).

The Romans

The Romans had a curiously popular amulet called a "fascinum." This was, essentially, an oversized erect phallus, sometimes with wings, typically worn around the neck—very obscene, indeed! However, it was thought that this very obscenity, along with the idea of the phallus being a sign of potency, would ward against evil and ill health. It was considered so powerful and so widely used that such amulets were even given to children by worried parents (Angel, 2013; Lóránt, 2016).

On top of this, the curse tablets named above by the Ancient Greeks continued to be popular following the colonization of Greece by the Roman empire (Blakemore, 2016).

The Ancient Egyptians

The Ancient Egyptians had many different

magickal symbols, just like the other cultures explored here. One item they used was akin to a magick wand formed out of hippopotamus ivory, which was used in childbirth magick as well as buried with the deceased for their protection in the afterlife (Larson, 2019). It was frequently carved with protective emblems associated with their gods, such as cats, frogs, lions, and serpents (Vink, 2016).

An interesting part of Ancient Egyptian magick is the role of sound. When completing a magickal ritual, one had to speak the correct words in the correct way, including the secret names of the deities called upon. It was also thought that causing a ruckus could drive away evil spirits—something that many witches do today, as well, calling it "sound cleansing," as I will explain in Chapters 4 and 6 (Pinch, 2011).

One type of popular amulet was made from papyrus (Dieleman, 2015). On this, a spell would be written out, and it would be rolled up and worn on a string around the neck— much more modest than the Roman fascinum!

Ancient West Asia and North Africa

In the empires of west Asia and north Africa (WANA), serpents were a potent symbol of protection, as indeed they were elsewhere in places like Greece, likely because of the cultural exchanges that these societies had. In Greece, the household spirit Agathos Daimon was often depicted as a snake and was thought to protect the people within the home. The WANA region went further than Greece, however, as it was deities within this area that featured characteristics of snakes. In particular, they, too, were typically seen as protectors of places rather than objects or people (Clark, n.d.; Golding, 2013).

Various ancient cultures of the WANA region also used "incantation bowls," sometimes called "demon bowls." These were basins decorated with a magickal inscription around the inside and buried upside down on the thresholds of the property. These were thought to trap evil spirits before they could enter (Murphy and Susalla, 2016).

Medieval Times

Despite the Christian culture that predominated by the time of the Medieval period, folk magick was still popular; indeed, it never died out, it just became syncretic with Christianity and its cosmology. This meant that pagan aspects were absorbed into Christianity in a complex way that involved both the keeping of some aspects of the old culture and the adaptation of others to fit the new worldview. We can see that this has happened with many other religions throughout history: The Romans did it with many of the cultures of the places they conquered, and enslaved Africans merged their own cultures with the Christianity taught to them on plantations to keep the magick alive, albeit in a slightly altered way.

During medieval times, however, there was a delineation between witches—who were thought to be casters of malefic magic—and the cunning folk, who were considered to be helpful and even thwarters of witchcraft (Baker, 2014). There were many charms and spells used to protect against a variety of different threats. I'll cover a few below to give an idea of the most prominent forms of protection during this time.

Witch Bottles

I have already mentioned witch bottles above, but it is worth discussing them in more detail because, in many ways, they are the precursor to the now very popular use of jar spells in modern witchcraft. A witch's bottle was a glass vessel filled with all sorts of sharp objects, such as bent pins, iron nails, and thorns. They were also filled with what is known as a "taglock," which consists of items that tie a spell to an individual (Morningbird, 2023). This included hair and nail clippings. Finally, once the bottle was filled with these items, it would be topped up with urine, sealed, and embedded in the building they were meant to protect. It was thought that the urine would draw the witch to the bottle and that the sharp objects would cause her harm (Meier, 2019). Some witches nowadays still construct these bottles—yes, including with the urine—but, instead, bury them on the four corners of their property.

Sheela Na Gig

Sheela Na Gigs are, like the Roman fascinum, a strange and overtly sexual protective symbol. Essentially, Sheela Na Gigs were carvings found across Britain and Ireland that depicted an old woman squatting and pulling her vulva wide open. Even more oddly, they were found on Romanesque churches! The true meaning of them is lost to time, but it is theorized that because the Devil could not stand the sight of a woman's genitals, his presence would be driven away (Harding, 2016).

The Curious Case of Cats in Walls

It's important to say that the following is not a practice that I endorse! During the Medieval period, dried cats were often found within the structure of buildings, specifically the roofs. It is thought that they were meant to deter not only evil but also rat and mouse infestation. Indeed, sometimes, they were posed with rats or mice to depict their role more fully, as if displaying to any wandering pests just what the feline's spirit would do to them (1196—Dried Cat, 2021).

Four Thieves' Vinegar

This is a concoction of legend; it is said that during the time of the Black Death, there was a band of thieves who robbed victims of the plague but never got sick themselves. This was because they had created what is known as Four Thieves' Vinegar, which they carried on their person to smell as well as douse themselves in. While recipes for the mixture abound, none can be verified as the true, original recipe. In fact, some include the use of poisonous herbs, so any recipes found should be followed with the care that all herbal remedies should be dealt with—after all, just because they're natural doesn't mean they're safe (Kelley, 2020).

Amulets, Charms, and Talismans

Before I proceed with the rest of the book, and particularly the spells, it is important to delineate some parts of vocabulary that are frequently used within witchcraft communities. It can be difficult to get to grips with the differences between amulets, charms, and talismans at first, but as knowledge is power, it is definitely worth doing so.

These definitions, however, are complicated by the fact that different practitioners of magick will define these objects differently. The definitions I proffer here are from a couple of sources, showing some agreement with the basics of what these items are. These definitions are as follows (Auryn, 2020b; Webster, 2004):

- **Charm:** Any object that you carry with you that is imbued with a certain magickal purpose. This can be for protection, as we will cover here, but also for other things such as attracting love or bringing luck. This can be confusing because sometimes short magickal sayings are also called charms. Neither is incorrect, but when discussing them it is important to give context for what you are talking about.

- **Amulet:** An item crafted to ward off certain influences. Typically, this will be to protect the carrier or wearer.
- **Talisman:** An item crafted to bring in certain influences. With protection in mind, this may be to supplement and amplify one's magickal potency.

What this shows us is that all amulets and talismans are charms, but not all charms will be both amulets and talismans; they'll be one or the other, depending on their desired function.

It should be noted that, in his book on the matter, Nigel Pennick (2021) defines amulets as being formed from natural materials, whereas talismans carry with them inscriptions or symbols that relate to their purpose. While I do not delineate the items in the same way, these definitions show some of the ways that these items are made: sourcing a natural object and changing it in some way to conform to your magickal will.

The Evil Eye

It would be nigh on impossible to speak about the cultural and historical beliefs surrounding self-defense against magickal and psychic threats without talking about the evil eye.

As noted above, the nazar is the famous blue, white, and black stylized eye that is often itself erroneously called the evil eye but is, in fact, a ward against it. So, what is it? The actual evil eye is a psychic attack transferred by an envious look. Sometimes, this is thought to be conferred on purpose, but other times, it is thought to occur by accident, simply through looking at someone with jealousy in your heart. The consequences of the attack are wide-ranging—to the point of being thought to bring downfall to the person affected (Hargitai, 2018; Schwarcz, 2022; Volandes, 2020).

Belief in the evil eye spans a wide variety of cultures, from the southern Mediterranean all the way up to northern Europe and into Britain. Thoughts on this attack date back to the 6th century B.C.E, being referenced by many famous Classical authors—including Plato—but have survived even through the Christianization of Europe (Hargitai, 2018; King, 2016; Schwarcz, 2022; Volandes, 2020).

Fortunately, as well as having been written about as a risk to the successful and prosperous since this time, amulets designed to avert the evil eye also have a long history, hence the ubiquity of the nazar among tourist shops in Greece, Cyprus, and Turkey. I will cover a way to develop an amulet that can be adapted to protect against the evil eye in more detail in Chapter 5, although the egg divination and cleanse in the next chapter will also help.

Ethics and Responsibilities

It is always important to know your values. They will guide you through life, and that includes through your witchcraft practice as well. However, not everyone believes the same things. I have already spoken about how magick is amoral, meaning it has no moral value in and of itself. Instead, it is a tool that can be harnessed for any number of ends. How you choose to use your magick is entirely up to you.

That said, there is a lot of debate in witchcraft communities about the morality of certain spells. Those considered baneful—including some protection spells and return-to-sender spells—get the most attention along with love spells, which I won't cover here in detail for reasons of space and lack of relevance to the topic at hand. I will instead outline below the two most common perspectives on these ethical controversies. This will put you in good stead to consider these further and see where your personal views align. It is not my place to lecture you on either of these points: So long as you fully understand the consequences of your actions, you are free to make your choices according to your own personal set of ethics.

Wicca and the Threefold Law

In Wicca, perhaps the most famous religion

featuring witchcraft, there are two doctrines that followers abide by. Firstly, there are the final two lines of the Wiccan Rede, the early version of which was written by famed witch Doreen Valiente in the 1960s. In the later, most quoted version, it states, "Eight words ye Wiccan Rede fulfill: An' it harm none, do what ye will" (Wigington, 2018c).

This is relatively easy to grasp, despite the stylistic choice of more Medieval language. The Rede is the basic guidance given to Wiccans, and it is summed up as allowing one to do whatever they wish, so long as it doesn't cause harm. This can be difficult to apply to life; as I stated previously, certain spells, even those considered to have "good" outcomes, will have unknown circumstances elsewhere. If you get a job, someone else doesn't. If you find money on the floor, it's fallen out of someone else's pocket. If you choose to follow the Rede, you must think through the possible consequences of your actions before acting and decide for yourself what "harm" here actually means.

The Threefold Law is the second part of the Wiccan code of ethics. It is also mentioned in the Rede and is stated as, "Mind the Threefold Law ye should, three times bad and three times good" (Wigington, 2018c). What this essentially means is that the moral outcomes of your actions should be paid attention to because the energy you direct outwards comes back to you three times. There is debate over whether or not this means one hit that is three times stronger or three separate instances. However, the general view is that this is a reason to not harm others because to do so invites harm unto yourself.

Not everyone who practices witchcraft follows the Rede or even believes in the principle of the Threefold Law. There is an argument to be made that energy cannot be multiplied, and so cannot come back three times, although some who make this argument do concede that sometimes circumstances will rebound back onto the witch in question, particularly if they do not do their due diligence in protecting themselves when casting baneful magick. However, since the beginnings of Wicca, there has been a strong moral argument made that one should not cause harm to another, and many do believe in the power of this Law. Indeed, this is a commonality among many world religions.

With respect to protection magick, Wiccans are allowed to look out for themselves—indeed, it could be argued that they should protect themselves if they wish to cause harm to none because that includes the self, too. However, certain spell types will not be used by a Wiccan, such as more aggressive wards and return-to-sender spells. This is because they would cause harm to whoever wishes to hurt the witch, and they do not believe in causing harm to a person, regardless of their intentions.

As not all witches are Wiccan, belief in the Rede and the Law is not a prerequisite to practicing witchcraft. However, if Wicca is a practice that interests you, it is worth researching the Rede further and considering how you think it operates and how it should be followed.

Moral Relativism and Gray Witchcraft

Moral relativism is a train of thought in philosophy that essentially states that there is no such thing as a universal set of principles or ethics that one should abide by. It points out that many of the things we consider right or wrong actually inhere from  our cultural perspective, which is a circumstance of birth. Some forms of moral relativism do note that some morals appear to be common among most cultures—such as murder being wrong—but even then, there may be nuances to how this is actually applied (Moral Relativism, 2022). For instance, many cultures will profess the evils of murder but will happily go to war, sending thousands to their deaths to cause injury to thousands of their enemies. Clearly, it isn't the killing that's decried but something else.

Many take the idea of moral relativism and apply it to reserving judgment about others' decisions—within reason, which will be limits applied by the individual reserving or dishing out the judgment. Many people also apply this to their own thoughts and actions, too. They argue that morality cannot be considered a static thing with hard and fast rules: Instead, the correct thing to do changes depending on the situation you find yourself in. Think, for example, about lying. Usually, we in Eurocentric cultures hold honesty in high regard, but when it comes to being asked by a friend, "Does my butt look big in this?" and it does, we'll often lie outright or fudge the truth a little to save their feelings.

This ties in with what is known as "gray

witchcraft." As the author of The Gray Witch's Grimoire, Amethyst Raine (2012) explains that gray witchcraft is about balance. It does not shy away from or fear darkness, for it recognizes that this is simply the shadow cast by light. Following on from this, gray witches will use techniques that are called "white" and "black" magick in common parlance to create balance within the world. They do not follow the rule of harming none because, to them, it is sometimes necessary to harm a person in order to protect someone else.

This is applying moral relativism to magick. It essentially shows that, again, magick is a tool to be wielded by someone and applied based on their own moral code. For the gray witch, this means that ethics are looser, being applied depending on the situation at hand. Many gray witches do not believe in the Threefold Law, but some accept that they may face consequences for their actions in some way, usually if they are not properly prepared or protected. However, it is up to the practitioner to weigh up the pros and cons of any action before performing their magick, including any ramifications to themselves. If this is a risk they are willing to take in order to create balance or avert a negative situation, they will go ahead with the planned spell.

When it comes to protection magick, for the gray witch, anything is permitted so long as it keeps a balance. This means they may engage in what others would call a "tit-for-tat," using aggressive wards that bite back against unwanted interferences or using a return-to-sender spell to teach a would-be curser a lesson. All is dependent on their own assessment of what is required in a particular situation. For example, if another witch appears to be a serial hexer, the gray witch may decide it is high time they experience a taste of their own medicine. However, if a spirit is merely curious, they will behave in a more gentle manner towards it when trying to remove its influence over a space.

Free Will and Coercion

Another concept that comes up a lot when discussing magickal ethics is free will. Many people who believe in the Wiccan Rede will say that anything is permitted so long as a person's free will is not impinged. Some witches who perform baneful magick will take a similar line when it comes to targeted love spells. This is because setting a spell upon someone in particular with the aim of causing them to love you means that you are altering their free will because you are forcing them to do something they otherwise didn't want to do.

For many, this is where they draw the line in their ethics, as they believe consent is necessary to perform magick—and even apply this to other, beneficial spells, such as healing, not wanting to do them for other people without their knowledge. Others do not mind doing any sort of spell; indeed, some make a career out of doing them.

Free will and harm can be tricky to discern the moral boundaries of. While you may not wish to impinge on someone's agency, there are circumstances where this may be ideal. For example, if someone is behaving in an abusive or harmful way, binding their actions will stop their behavior at the cost of their free will, but if it's the only way to prevent greater harm, a morally relativist gray witch may take this action. Again, the issue of free will is something to consider for your own witchcraft practice.

Karma

Ah, karma: a word thrown about a lot when talking about spiritual ethics, but one which is deeply misunderstood. Many people talk about karma as the consequences of someone's actions in this life. You'll often hear people say of a harmful person that karma will bite them in the butt at some point. It is treated as the "just desserts" someone gets based on their good or bad behavior.

However, the concept of karma originally comes from Indian philosophy in religions such as Hinduism and Buddhism. As the latter, in particular, has spread out across the world, many of us have learned this word but misconstrued it. Karma, instead of being the thing delivered upon you in this life, is the law that governs what your existence will be like in the next life. You almost accrue it by the actions you carry out in this life, good or bad, and then, when it comes to being reincarnated—an important concept in these religions—karma determines the many different circumstances that you will be born into. As such, it is a call to live life morally—according to the precepts of the religion in question—as well as an explanation for why your life is how it currently is (Olivelle, 2023).

You can be a witch and believe in karma; indeed, many pagans believe in some kind of reincarnation, and so, the belief in karma may make sense to you in  terms of how certain lives are allotted to certain souls. However, it is important to know what it actually is, otherwise, we are doing the cherrypicking and bastardizing of cultures that I warned about in the introduction to this book. It is always good to be mindful of this and to use the proper terms. While you may believe that the energy people give out comes back to them in this life in some way, it is better to say that than to misuse a term with a very specific meaning dating back hundreds of years, debated thoroughly within a deep philosophical tradition.

CHAPTER 2
IDENTIFYING CURSES, HEXES, AND PSYCHIC ATTACKS

In Witchcraft, each of us must reveal our own truth. – Starhawk

Before you can even start thinking about reversal magick, you've got to first figure out what exactly it is you're reversing.

This information will put you in good stead for the remaining chapters of the book. You must be clear on what it is you're trying to prevent, reverse, or banish before doing any magick as you always want to be precise in your casting. This is because it is better to direct your energy to one point at a time, rather than throwing it out willy-nilly, as you will then have more control over the consequences of the spell and its efficacy can be measured more easily.

You should always first rule out mundane influence—that is, the non-magickal—before jumping to the conclusion that you are the victim of baneful magick or psychic attack. This will be covered more below in the section *Distinguishing Between Natural Events and Magickal Interference.* This is because, fortunately, it is much more likely for an "attack" to actually be something non-supernatural instead.

However, if after this analysis, you are still concerned that you have come under attack in some way, you'll need to know what sort of attack it is. This is what I will cover in the first section below, as there is indeed a difference between curses, hexes, and jinxes, as well as psychic attacks from elsewhere. I'll then outline what the warning signs of these types of attack are so that you can be aware of them should they come about. Finally, after a trip down the lane of discernment, I'll cover the ways that you can find out, through divination, if you have indeed been attacked, ending with an understanding of the longer-term effects of these psychic injuries.

Curses, Hexes, Jinxes, and Psychic Attacks: What's the Difference?

It can be a bit confusing to discern the differences between psychic and magickal attacks, particularly because they can share symptoms and effects. However, there is indeed a difference between curses, hexes, and jinxes—which are magickal attacks—and psychic attacks. Knowing what sort of attack you have come under allows you to reverse it much more easily. In some cases, a simple cleansing of yourself or a space will be required, whereas others may warrant a more labor-intensive spell to undo their influence. Knowing what is necessary prevents you from expending too much of your own energy on ineffective and inefficient actions.

Curses, Hexes, and Jinxes

Let's first talk about the similarities between curses, hexes, and jinxes. All of these can be called "baneful" magick, meaning that they are cast with malicious intent to harm. As Glinda Porter (2021) writes, it is impossible to perform any of these unintentionally—to confer any of these effects in such a way would instead be considered a psychic attack. This is because any of these actions are spells, which require the intent and focused energetic exertion of the caster.

Another similarity is that all of these spells can be placed on not just individuals but also groups, places, and objects. We often hear stories about places carrying a curse if one disrespects it, such as a graveyard, and there are often urban legends about cursed dolls and suchlike. While it is likely to be more common to send these sorts of spells against an individual or their family, it is worth bearing these similarities in mind.

When it comes to the differences, however, we can speak in terms of how "serious" the injury caused by the spell is and how long it lasts. The blog Tea and Rosemary outlines this well, and so, the information below is, in part, based on their account of these (*Curses, hexes, and jinxes: What's the difference?*, 2020).

A jinx is a short-lived spell that is relatively harmless, causing minor annoyance. For example, you could cast a spell on someone so that they keep stubbing their toe on any table they walk past for a day or send them nightmares one night.

A hex is more harmful and lasts somewhat longer than a jinx. Often, a caster will set it to last until the person who's been hexed has learned their lesson, whatever that may be.

The longest it will last is perhaps a whole season. An example of a hex would be to cause the individual to ruminate on and regret their actions, particularly if it was a spell to get justice, as many hexes nowadays are. Another example may be to cause ruin in one specific area of their life. Social media sites like TikTok abound with videos of hexes performed to remove someone's sexual prowess, for want of a better, PG-13 term, usually as an act of revenge.

A curse, however, is the most harmful of all and can last a lifetime—sometimes even longer, if we're discussing generational curses. The harm caused can be absolutely dire; indeed, there are many folktales and urban legends of curses causing someone to die in a tragic way. The impact of each curse will vary, but we can get an idea of them via some examples, such as a curse to destroy all hopes of a relationship or career or a curse to return the hurt caused by a person onto themselves. This is another reason why these spells are sometimes used for a sense of justice; there is much talk in online witch communities of cursing abusers, for instance.

Because curses are used in the worst-case scenario, they are quite rare. Most of the spells we hear about as "curses" are in fact a hex or even "just" a jinx. This will have an impact on how we will go about dismantling such spells, as less energy and focus are required to break a hex than a full-blown curse.

Types of Psychic Attack

The College of Psychic Studies notes, "it is probable that we have each experienced a psychic attack at some point in our life, whether we are aware of it or not" (*What Is a Psychic Attack?*, 2022). This is because psychic attacks, unlike baneful magick, can be performed unintentionally. An example of this, the evil eye, was covered in the last chapter, wherein we saw that many cultures believe psychic attacks to often be unintentionally cast by a jealous gaze.

So, what is a psychic attack? Essentially, there are two kinds: Firstly, it can be the conference of negative energy from one person to another, as we see in the evil eye example. The second kind is the sapping of energy from one being into another. We see this in the example of what are called "energy" or "psychic vampires," who may not even know themselves to be one but still "feed" from the energy of others (Konstantinos, 2002).

It is easier to psychically attack those we are close with because we already share some form of energetic bond (*What Is a Psychic Attack?*,

2022). Again, this is frequently unintentional: Discussing intense emotions can be draining, but that doesn't mean we should neglect the emotional needs of our loved ones and not comfort them when they're down. Instead, we can use a shield to protect our energy from becoming drained during these situations, something I cover in Chapter 4.

This is particularly important for those who are empaths—people who feel the emotions of another person and know exactly what they're feeling because of this. While being an empath can be an amazing gift, it also often results in quite a bit of fatigue. If this is you, it is very important to learn how to shield and perhaps create a protective amulet in order to conserve your own energy.

A psychic attack tends not to last very long,

and we will typically regain this energy ourselves over a period of time. We can help ourselves to regain energy by cleansing, grounding through connection to the earth and heavenly bodies' energy, and doing restful activities. We'll cover these more in the fourth chapter.

Nonhuman Causes of Psychic Attacks

It is not only other humans who can threaten our energy, however. We share our world with a variety of different autonomous spirits and entities, both human and nonhuman. Most are happy to live and let live, getting on with their own lives and not bothering us unless we choose to try and contact them ourselves. They're like other people with their own business going on, essentially.

Some entities, on the other hand, do actively engage with us, particularly if we have (perhaps latent) psychic abilities or practice witchcraft. Many of these spirits will be helpful, wanting to work with you to achieve your magickal goals and teach you more so that you advance along your path. These are commonly called "spirit guides," and such relationships can be incredibly meaningful. Unfortunately, however, a very small minority of spirits do not have kind intentions and so may decide to take it upon themselves to inflict psychic damage against a witch.

I cannot emphasize enough that this is a very rare occurrence indeed. Tales of demonic possession and poltergeists wreaking havoc in a house are almost always explained by mundane causes, of which there are many. However, as this book aims at being a comprehensive guide to self-defensive magick, it is only right to mention the rare and the weird so that you have a well-rounded knowledge of psychic and magickal threats. It is beyond the scope of this book to delve deeper into the types of entities known to occasionally cause chaos, but suffice it to say it isn't just demons—indeed, it very, very rarely is. However, it is possible to do further research into this if it is an area that interests you. That said, what I can cover in the space of this book are techniques to protect yourself from unwanted spirits, as well as the basics of banishing. Both of these topics will be covered in later chapters.

The Signs of Hexes and Psychic Attacks

Because hexes and curses can target a number of different things, the possible signs of them are quite vast. Psychic attacks can also vary. However, all of these have some similarities in the form of the most common symptoms they bring. These are (*What Is a Psychic Attack?*, 2022; *"Am I cursed?" 10 symptoms of magickal danger,* n.d.; Thorne, 2022)

- extended bouts of ongoing bad luck or failure in one specific area of life
- becoming more accident-prone or more accidents happening around you for an ongoing period of time
- lack of energy
- depression, erratic mood, and suicidal thoughts, when this is unusual for you
- chronic health issues that have no known medical cause, such as joint pain, headaches, and frequent nausea
- stress for no apparent reason
- vivid, recurring nightmares
- sexual dysfunction of some kind or another
- feeling uncomfortable in certain places, especially if they are also avoided by children or pets
- strange, unexplainable happenings in the home, such as pictures falling off the wall or your keys being moved about
- relationship difficulties and repeated arguments, including with partners,

family, and friends, with no apparent cause—just tension and conflict arising easily, with quick, heated tempers

- people avoiding you or becoming more indifferent to you
- decreased creativity, particularly if one is usually a creative sort
- uncharacteristic compulsions to do certain things, or acting out of character, in general
- bad omens`

Distinguishing Between Natural Events and Magickal Interference

As you will notice, many of the above symptoms of magickal and psychic attacks could have perfectly rational explanations. There is a saying that gets passed around quite a lot in witchcraft communities: "Mundane over magickal." This means that we should always look first for causes that are non-magickal which could explain certain phenomena. Another way of putting it might be "don't jump to (magickal) conclusions."

More often than not, with some thinking about the phenomena you are experiencing, there will be a material cause. This is because things like magickal attacks, hauntings, and ongoing psychic attacks are all quite rare phenomena. While it is wonderful to experience the magickal in our everyday lives and see the vast interconnectedness of the universe and its inhabitants, we should be wary of assigning occult meaning to everything because this can lead down a tricky road of paranoia, among other problems.

So, how do you go about discerning whether or not your experiences are caused by magick? Well, depending on what's going on for you, the questions you need to ask yourself will be different. Below is an inexhaustive list of the sorts of questions you may need to ask yourself. These may then break down into even more questions, but it is important to follow these lines of inquiry so that you have fully ruled out all logical explanations. Some of the questions you may ask are as follows:

- Is there a medical explanation for my physical or emotional symptoms? To fully explore this option, you will need to go to an actual doctor or other medical professional trained in the area of your particular issue.

- Have I been exposing myself to too much stress? Consider whether or not you are coping well with your responsibilities, if you are trying to fit too much into your days, or if anything has happened recently that could be causing anxiety, fatigue, or other symptoms.

- Is this really out of the ordinary? Some things may seem strange, but when we think about them in more detail, we begin to see that actually they're quite normal. An example of this, to make it clearer, is seeing a particular type of bird associated with a deity regularly and, at first, thinking it is a sign, until you realize it is because of the migratory or mating patterns of that species at that time of year.

- Is this really happening that much more than usual? Consider the frequency and duration of the phenomena you have been experiencing. It could simply be confirmation bias: Once an idea has popped into your head, you begin to notice it everywhere and think it's more common than it is because you simply didn't notice it before.

- Could this be caused by carbon monoxide

poisoning or other environmental factors? It might sound strange, but carbon monoxide leaking into an environment can cause all sorts of strange symptoms, and a cursory internet search pulls up multiple instances of it being the source of what were thought to be hauntings.

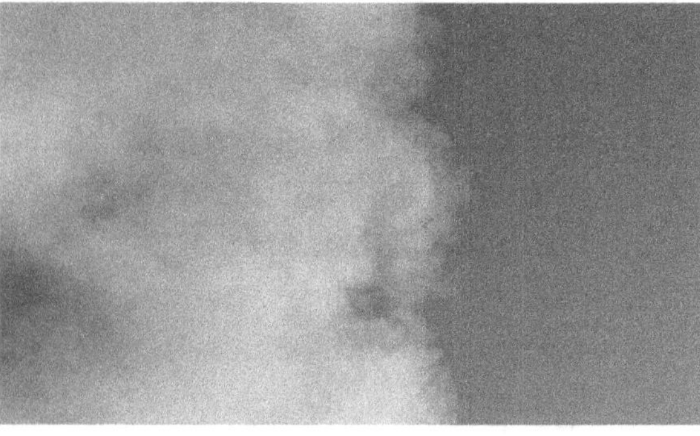

- Did this happen suddenly or has it been brewing for some time? This might equally apply to a variety of different phenomena, from a progressive worsening of health to the dissolution of a relationship.

- Could this be the result of unresolved trauma? Spiritual bypassing is a psychological defense mechanism that prevents us from having to deal with hard truths about ourselves by assigning a magickal cause to certain symptoms and phenomena when, in fact, the cause is unresolved issues and traumas. If you think this is the case, consider delving into this in more detail, potentially with the support of a mental health professional such as a trustworthy therapist.

- Am I a forgetful person who lives with other people, and so, might that be why it seems things keep moving by themselves? You may very well be forgetting where you put your keys, or you keep leaving them in strange places where your roomies will find and move them.

- Has my child, family member, pet, or other loved one experienced something recently that could have caused them to behave in this way? Fireworks and loud storms may make pets frightened—and sometimes children, too. Family members may be going through stresses of their own and so may act out of character. There may also be underlying health issues to consider—another reason why it may be good to consult a medical or veterinary specialist.

Using Divination to Uncover Hidden Curses, Hexes, and Attacks

Divination isn't just about trying to predict what the future may hold. It can also be used to uncover hidden information. Because of this, you can use it to find out if you are under attack in some way. Before introducing some ways to do this, however, I should make two points.

Firstly, you don't need to be psychic in the sense of common parlance to use divination methods like those listed below. While being claircognizant—able to know, without mundane means, information that you would not otherwise know—would be extremely handy in this and other scenarios, it is not essential for divination. Tools to connect to the energies that surround us and are within us will mean you can uncover the necessary information. However, if you are still worried about your abilities, you can find a (reputable) reader of various methods online to commission a reading.

Secondly, because a lot is at stake when it comes to psychic or magickal attack, it would be a good idea to double-check any readings, preferably using different methods. In these situations, it is good to try a "yes/no" means of answering questions as well as one that is more descriptive—for example, a pendulum reading backed up by Tarot, which I explain below. This will mean that you'll be able to better discern the accuracy of the reading and know for certain what has transpired. You may also double-check by asking someone else to perform a reading for you.

With all that said, I'll now go through three of the more common ways of divining for hexes and psychic attacks. This is not an exhaustive list, however. If you find another divinatory system more helpful, then I would say to use that. Everyone's ability to tap into their intuition is different, and so, different methods word better for different people.

Pendulum

Pendulums are often crystals hanging from a chain, but anything that hangs can be used as a pendulum, whether that's a treasured ring dangling from a necklace or a stone with a hole in it attached to some string. They are popular for all sorts of questions that can 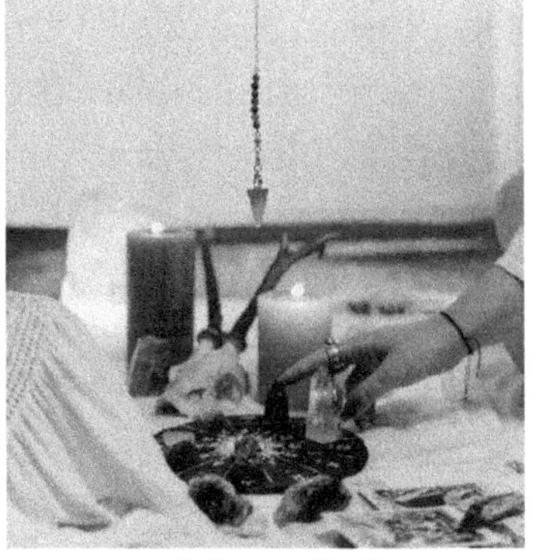 be answered with a yes or no, although there are ways to get a "maybe" from them too.

There are a couple of ways to divine with a pendulum. The easiest is with a pendulum board. These can be found cheaply online or created at home. You would plot out a circle divided up into eighths. One line (usually the vertical) would have "yes" at either end, another "no" (usually the horizontal), and the remaining ones would be "maybe" and "ask again." You can then dangle the pendulum steadily over the board and ask your questions, using the movements to come to your answer.

Another way—one that does not rely on a board—is to capture the pendulum's natural calibrations (Thorne, 2020). To do this, you would ask the pendulum to show you how it moves for each answer. You would then test this with questions you already know the answer to, such as "Is my name X?" "Am I a woman?" or "Do I live in X town?". Once you are certain you have ascertained how the pendulum moves for each possible answer, you may proceed to ask it yes/no questions about your current malady to find out what ails you.

Tarot and Oracle Cards

Not all oracle cards are Tarot, but all Tarot could be called a type of oracle card, for these are decks of cards containing symbols that, when interpreted, can tell you more meaningful and nuanced answers than is possible with a pendulum.

Cartomancy—as divination by cards is called—is decades old and a very popular means to uncover information. Tarot is the most famous of these cartomancy methodologies. Composed of a deck of 78 cards, it started off during the early modern period as a game, but by the 1780s, it came to be adapted for fortune-telling (Parlett, 1999). The most famous imagery for Tarot is those derived from the Rider Waite Smith deck, created at the turn of the 20th century and popular to this day (*The Rider Waite Smith Deck*, n.d.).

It is well beyond the scope of this book to go into the meanings of the various cards, but there are many books and online resources for this—indeed, as I said previously, I have written one myself (Visconti, 2019). However, it is possible to outline here a spread that will be of use when divining about attacks. A spread is when cards are laid out in a specific order relating to certain questions, with the cards then interrogated individually according to how the symbolism answers the question; this is then analyzed to see the relationship between cards and what this says about the situation as a whole.

A simple three-card layout that is a standard one in a Tarot reader's roster is as follows: Laid out in a horizontal line, the first card represents the source of a problem, the second its effect, and the third its solution. Check the meaning of the card for each question, sure, but also try to come to your own understanding of the answer. What does the card intuitively feel like it is telling you? What is the symbolism of the card saying? Its colors, layout, and motifs? Take some time to ponder the cards, and write down your interpretation so that you do not forget it. The benefits of this spread are that it can give you an idea of how to rid yourself of the current problem on top of confirming if you are under a spell or psychic attack.

Oomancy: Divination With Eggs

A previously fairly unheard-of method of

divination, oomancy—divination using eggs (yes, you read that correctly)—has exploded in popularity due to discussions on social media sites such as TikTok. Combining both a form of divining about curses as well as a way to cleanse and remove them, the method is known within the Latine Brujería community as *"limpia."* However, similar rituals can be found in other folk magick traditions.

Eggs work for this because they are considered empty vessels (Alejandrez-Prasad, 2023). The ritual can remove curses in some instances because the egg absorbs it, but even if the curse requires another spell to break it, the egg will be able to tell if there is a hex present.

So, how do you do it? First, fetch your egg, a cup with some cold, salted water or incense for cleansing in it, an empty, clear cup, and a candle, and find a place where you'll be able to concentrate. Then, there are several stages involved in this ritual, which I will lay out step-by-step (Alejandrez-Prasad, 2023):

1. Pray your intentions over the egg while holding it. Fill it with your energy to connect with it while telling it what you need it to do. Invoke a deity if you so wish (something I'll cover more in Chapter 3).

2. Cleanse the egg. You can use the salt water for this or smoke cleanse it by waving protective incense all around it (I'll cover protective herbs in Chapter 3, too, and cleansing in Chapter 4).

3. Fill the empty cup to about 75% full of cold water, and light your candle.

4. Run the egg over your entire body, top to bottom. Do so gently, so as not to crack it. Do this several times, until you feel intuitively that you have done enough. You may repeat your intentions or pray as you do this.

5. Crack your egg into the cup, and place the eggshell to one side. Take photos so that you can refer back to them if necessary.

6. Read the egg using the interpretations below.

7. Dispose of the egg—not in the trash, but either down the sink or flushed down the toilet.

To read the egg, you will need to consider how it sits in the water. There are many ways it may hold up in the fluid. Interpretations of these are as follows (Alejandrez-Prasad, 2023; Brethauer, 2023):

- **Bubbles:** Small bubbles signify a successful cleanse, whereas big ones suggest gossip and being watched.

- **Foam:** There are things brewing beneath the surface that you are currently unaware of. Further divination may prove useful here.
- **Cloudiness:** Cloudiness like a gray mist over the yolk represents physical symptoms that require focus and must be lifted.
- **Water remains clear:** Things are going well—no need to be concerned!
- **Strings:** These come top-to-bottom and represent "cords" connecting you to others that need to be cut. They may also represent worries, particularly if there are many of them and you are feeling anxious. Basically, they are signs of negative energy still affecting you.

- **Cages:** These enclose the yolk, are big, and are usually egg-shaped themselves. They symbolize feeling closed in and trapped.
- **Spikes:** These come bottom-to-top and represent negative energy being released.
- **Cobwebs:** General negativity that we

pick up in our day-to-day lives. A simple cleanse should do the trick.

- **An eye:** The evil eye has been placed upon you and needs to be removed.
- **A face:** This represents someone who has cursed you.
- **Other symbols:** Sometimes, you may see other, rarer symbols in the egg, which can be also interpreted; guides for symbols can be bought or found online— something relating to dreams or tea leaf readings would be helpful.
- **Egg shell in glass:** Be sure this isn't just because you cracked the egg badly! However, if there is shell, it can reveal that the situation is overwhelming even the ritual and will require further action.
- **Blood in the yolk:** Something needs to be healed, or a hex needs to be broken. Consider further divination to find out what it is, exactly.
- **Yolk doesn't sink to the bottom:** A symbol of a curse or attack of some kind.
- **Broken yolk:** There is an attack or negativity against you that has "broken open" and is currently having an effect on you. It will need to be released.
- **Double yolk:** A good omen! While it can

mean twins, it is generally a sign of prosperity (due to the connection to fertility).

As you can see, sometimes, the egg itself is sufficiently cleansing on its own to rid you of negativity. However, it can also reveal a need for further investigation—hence my call to you to always double-check—or further action. This is what I will cover in the following chapters, after taking a brief detour to talk about the building blocks necessary to construct and carry out spells, such as what herbs and crystals correspond to protection.

CHAPTER 3
TOOLS AND INGREDIENTS FOR REVERSAL AND PROTECTION SPELLS

You are the most powerful tool in your life. Use your energy, your thoughts, and your magick wisely! – Dacha Avalin

Before it is possible to look at means of protection, reversal, and banishing, it is necessary to understand the elements that will comprise these spells. Different ingredients will correspond to different magickal ends. "Correspondence" here means the properties of a herb, crystal, oil, or other ingredient in relation to its magickal uses. It is also pertinent to understand the importance of timing in your spell work because different moon phases and days of the week have different properties, too. As well as this, I will run through the most common tools used in witchcraft so that you know what sort of things you should gradually build a collection of. Finally, although it is possible to have a secular witchcraft practice, many people choose to work with deities, spirits, and ancestors in their craft, so I'll go through the basics of this, too. However, it is good to first understand the roles of the different elements in witchcraft.

The Use of Elements

Most witchcraft in the West uses the classical four elements as a basis for their craft. These are earth, air, fire, and water. They have the four cardinal directions mapped to them: North is earth, east is air, fire is south, and water is west. Many witches will use a compass to place their working altar in one of the directions for different spells according to what they are trying to achieve so that they are facing the appropriate direction when working their magick. This is because each element rules over different aspects of life (Beyer, 2019; Saint Thomas, 2020; Wigington, 2019b):

- **Earth:** Associated with fertility and prosperity, earth is a very stable element that relates strongly to the materiality of the world around us. In Tarot, it rules over the Suit of Pentacles (sometimes called the Suit of Coins). In astrology, it rules over the signs Taurus, Virgo, and Capricorn. In alchemical terms, it is cold and dry, as well as carrying feminine or receptive energies. It is associated with the colors green and brown.

- **Air:** Corresponding to all areas of communication, air is associated with the rational mind. In astrology, it rules over Aquarius, Libra, and Gemini. In Tarot, it is associated with the Suit of Swords. In alchemical terms, it is warm and moist and carries masculine or active energies. It is associated with the color yellow.

- **Fire:** Associated with protection and all kinds of strength and courage, fire relates to the will. In alchemy, it is warm and dry and also carries masculine or active energy. In astrology, it rules over Aries, Leo, and Sagittarius, and in Tarot, the Suit of Wands. It is associated with the colors orange and red.

- **Water:** Healing, cleansing, and purifying, water rules over emotions and intuition. In astrology, it commands Pieces, Cancer, and Scorpio, and it is associated with the Suit of Cups in Tarot. It is moist and cold in alchemy, as well as carrying feminine or receptive energies. It is associated with the color blue.

There is one more element to consider,

however: spirit. This fifth element is sometimes also known as "ether" or "quintessence." It does not have formalized correspondences as the other elements do, but it is instead the energy or essence that suffuses everything in the universe and connects us with what is around us. It also helps us to connect

with the spiritual realms (Beyer, 2019).

You might even say that it is the manipulation of the spirit within us, our ingredients, and the wider world that allows magick to work. This is, of course, just a theory—as there is no singularly known way to understand the workings of magick—but one that many practitioners subscribe to.

However, we don't necessarily invoke spirit as we do many of the other elements. With these, they are frequently called to help with magick in a process known as "calling in the quarters." There are many different mythical beings that have associations with different elements, including archangels, the fae, and elementals. There are also those known as the

Watchtowers or the Guardians of the elements. Traditionally, they are called upon in Wiccan ways of laying a magickal circle during spell work or ritual—something we cover in a more simple, accessible form in Chapter 5. However, suffice it to say that you can invoke the powers of the elements in your magick if you so wish to add potency to your spells. One way to do this is by figuring out what element a herb relates to, as different plants have been ascribed different elemental energies based on their appearance. This practice can be included in protection magick.

The Tools of the Trade

There are a number of tools that are common in witchcraft that it is important to familiarize yourself with. Many of these are used for ritual purposes in religions like Wicca, but they also each serve both magickal and practical functions and act as powerful symbols for certain concepts. The common tools of the witch are as follows (Alexander, 2014; Chamberlain, 2017b):

- **Wand:** Yes, magick isn't about fairytale witches, but the notion of a magick wand had to come from somewhere; the wand is indeed a common tool of witches. Wands are used to draw down and direct energy during spell casting and can be used when casting magickal circles, which I will go into more detail about in Chapter 5. Wands correspond to the element of fire. Traditionally, the wand is made from wood, but nowadays, it can be fashioned from a variety of materials, including crystal. Many witches will find their own wand in nature—not by cutting wood from a tree, which would be impolite unless the tree's spirit agrees to it, but by sourcing sticks from the ground. While it is not essential, many wands are also customized by the owner, such as with carvings of runes and sigils.

- **Athame:** A blunt ritual dagger, traditionally double-sided and with a black handle, the athame is also used for directing energy. Sometimes, it is used for cutting through energy. It is associated with the element air.

- **Pentacle:** A symbol associated with Wicca as a religion but also with the element earth in magick, in general, the pentacle is a five-pointed star—one point at the top—with a circle around it; it is a pentagram if it is without the circle. In magick, it is used for charging items and is also a potent symbol of protection itself.

- **Chalice:** Associated quite naturally with the element water, the chalice is a vessel dedicated to holding liquids for ritual activity. In Wicca, it is common to end magickal and ritual practices with some food and drink (traditionally small cakes and ale), and so, this is the most common use for chalices. However, you may use a specially demarcated tea cup if a spell requires the drinking of a herbal tea—and always remember to use herbs safely!

- **Cauldron:** Also associated with the element water, a cauldron should be made from a fire-resistant material (traditionally iron) and have a lid that can smother flames if necessary. It is used to safely burn incense or spell materials.

While you don't need to run out straight away and amass all of the tools listed above, it is worth knowing what the most common ones are in witchcraft and gradually building up your collection of these. When you first begin, it is enough to use what is at hand, but over time, it is nice to gather together items specifically only used as tools of magick. This helps you to draw a demarcation between everyday life and the sacred, bringing you closer to your craft when you engage with these objects and making it easier to enter into a mindset conducive to casting magick.

Essential Herbs, Crystals, and Oils for Defense

Spells almost always need ingredients. Like the elements, each ingredient has its own correspondences—properties that can be drawn on to affect the change you want to see in the world. By working with these ingredients in your spell, you can harness their energy to supplement your own, shaping it with your intention toward your desired end. This will become clearer in the later chapters.

For now, let's take a look at some herbs and crystals that correspond to the intentions you'll have around protection, cleansing, banishing, and hex-breaking. Once this is done, I will then discuss how oils can be used safely as a different means of harnessing the power of herbs.

Herbs

Below are some common and easy-to-obtain herbs that can be used in defensive magick. A word of caution, however: You should not ingest or burn any herb without first doing your due diligence on whether or not it is safe. While herbs are the bounty of nature, this does not mean they are always safe to work with in every way. There are many guides available about this online or in books.

As well as their magickal properties, I will include some other information about other associations you can draw on. I'll list the feminine/receptive or masculine/projective properties, what element the plant is associated with, and what planet they are associated with, as this is one way to bring different forms of energy into your work by drawing on celestial and elemental power.

Some herbs you may begin to work with once you've done your due diligence are as follows (Cunningham, 2007):

- **Aloe vera:** A feminine/receptive plant associated with the moon and the element water. It is used for protection.

- **Ash:** A fiery plant that is masculine/protective and associated with the sun. It is used for protection.
- **Basil:** A masculine/projective, fiery plant associated with Mars and used for protection and banishing.
- **Bay/Laurel:** Another fiery masculine/projective plant used for protection, cleansing, banishing, and hex-breaking.
- **Beans:** Associated with air and the planet Mercury, beans are all masculine/projective and can be used for protection and banishing.
- **Birch:** A watery, feminine/receptive plant, birch is associated with the planet Venus. It can be used for cleansing, banishing, and protection.
- **Cactus:** The associations of cacti vary due to them being a classification of  plants, but all can have their spines used for protection.
- **Cedar:** Another fiery masculine/projective tree associated with the sun, it can be used for cleansing

and protection.

- **Chamomile:** A watery masculine/projective plant that can be used for many things, such as protection, cleansing, and hex-breaking.
- **Chili:** Unsurprisingly associated with fire, chili peppers are ruled by the planet Mars and are masculine/projective. They can be used for hex-breaking.
- **Cinnamon:** Yet another projective/masculine plant associated with fire and, this time, the sun, cinnamon is used for protection.
- **Clove:** A masculine/projective plant associated with fire and the planet Jupiter, it can be used for banishing and protection.
- **Coconut:** A feminine/receptive plant, coconut is associated with water and the moon, and it can be used for cleansing and protection.
- **Cotton:** Another feminine/receptive plant associated with the moon, this plant corresponds with the earth element, and it can be used for protection.
- **Cumin:** This masculine/projective herb, cumin, is associated with Mars and fire. It is used for protection and banishing.

- **Dragon's Blood:** A resin commonly used in incense blends, you can probably already infer from Dragon's Blood's name that it'll be a fiery plant. It is also masculine/projective and associated with Mars. You can draw on its power for protection and banishing.
- **Eucalyptus:** A feminine/receptive plant associated with water and the moon. It can be used for protection.
- **Fern:** Associated with Mercury and air, ferns are also projective/masculine in their energies. They are used for protection and banishing.
- **Frankincense:** We're back to fire and the sun with frankincense. It, too, is masculine/projective and used for protection, banishing, and cleansing.
- **Garlic:** A projective/masculine plant, garlic is fiery and associated with Mars. It is used for protection and banishing.
- **Geranium:** A watery plant associated with Venus, it is feminine/receptive. It is used for protection.
- **Heather:** Another feminine/receptive plant associated with water and Venus, it can be used for protection.
- **Holly:** A masculine/projective plant

associated with Mars and fire, it is used for protection.

- **Ivy:** A feminine/receptive plant, ivy is associated with water and Saturn. It is used for protection.
- **Juniper:** Associated with the sun, fire, and masculine/projective energies, juniper is used for banishing and protection.
- **Lavender:** A masculine/projective plant associated with air and the planet Mercury, lavender is used for protection and cleansing.
- **Lemon:** Another feminine/receptive plant, lemon is associated with water and the moon; lemon can be used for cleansing.

- **Lime:** Associated with the sun, lime is fiery and masculine/projective. It is used for protection and hex-breaking.

- **Marjoram:** A masculine/projective yet airy plant associated with Mercury. Marjoram can be used for protection.
- **Mugwort:** Another feminine/receptive plant, mugwort is associated with Venus and the element earth. It is used for protection.
- **Nettle:** Back to masculine/projective, now. As anyone who has been stung by a nettle will not be surprised to learn, it is associated with fire and the planet Mars. It is excellent at protection, hex-breaking, and banishing.
- **Oak:** A fiery tree that is both masculine/projective and associated with the sun, it is used for protection.
- **Olive:** Associated with the fiery sun, olive is also masculine/projective and used for protection.
- **Onion:** Masculine/projective and fiery, onion is associated with Mars and used for protection and banishing.
- **Parsley:** An airy plant associated with Mercury, parsley is masculine/projective, too. It is used for protection and cleansing.
- **Peony:** A masculine/projective plant

associated with fire and the sun, it can be used for banishing and projection.

- **Pepper:** Unsurprisingly fiery, pepper is masculine/projective and also associated with Mars. It is used for protection, hex-breaking, and cleansing.
- **Peppermint:** Associated with fire but also the planet Mercury, peppermint is masculine/projective and good for cleansing.
- **Pine:** An airy plant associated with Mars, pine is a masculine/projective ingredient useful for protection, cleansing, and banishing.
- **Rice:** Another plant related to air, but this time sun, rice is also masculine/projective. It can be used for protection.
- **Rose:** A feminine/receptive plant unsurprisingly associated with Venus and water, rose—in particular, its thorns—can be used for protection.
- **Rosemary:** Good for protection, banishing, and cleansing, rosemary is a fiery Mars-linked plant that is projective/masculine.
- **Garden sage:** Associated with Jupiter and the element air, sage is a masculine/projective plant used for

protection and cleansing. This should not be confused with white sage, the use of which is a closed Indigenous practice.

- **Sandalwood (white):** Back to a feminine/receptive plant, sandalwood is associated with water and the moon. It is used for banishing and protection.
- **Thistle:** Used for hex-breaking, protection, banishing, and cleansing, thistle is a projective/masculine plant. It is associated with fire and Mars.
- **Thyme:** A feminine/receptive plant associated with Venus and water, it can be used for cleansing.
- **Valerian:** A watery plant associated with Venus, it is feminine/receptive and used for protection and cleansing.
- **Vervain:** A receptive/feminine plant associated with Venus and earth, vervain is used for cleansing, banishing, and protection.

You don't need to rush out and buy all these herbs at once. However, this should act as a short guide to some herbs you can use in rituals and spells and allow you to substitute one for another if need be. You can also do more research into the uses of these herbs historically, within folk magick, and within herbalism to find out more about them.

Crystals

As with the above, this is but a list for beginners to become acquainted with some of the crystals and rocks that you can use in your defensive magick and is in no way supposed to be totally comprehensive. Again, each one of these stones can be researched further, and you needn't rush out to buy them all immediately. Small chips and tumble stones can, however, be purchased at low prices and will work just as well as that great, big, several-hundred-dollar hunk of quartz. So, without further ado, here is a short list of protective gems (Cunningham, 2021):

- agate (banded, black, and brown)
- amethyst
- carnelian.
- clear quartz
- coral
- flint
- garnet
- jade
- jet

- lapis lazuli
- malachite
- marble
- obsidian
- onyx
- petrified wood
- pumice
- red jasper
- sunstone
- tiger's eye
- tourmaline (red and black)
- turquoise

Additionally, the use of stones can be implemented in many ways. For instance, aquamarine can be used for purification and pumice for banishment.

The Safe and Proper Use of Oils

People sometimes have a perception that everything natural is harmless. I've already cautioned against ingesting and burning herbs you are unfamiliar with because this widespread belief simply isn't the case. These words of warning also apply to essential oils, which are created by condensing the oils of a plant down to create a chemical that can be harmful if not used correctly.

I am not trying to scare you off from using

essential oils, however. There are ways to do this safely, and many witches find them useful in their craft. You can create oil blends yourself quite safely at home to use in magick, typically for anointing the self or consecrating ritual objects.

So, it is perfectly possible to add essential oils into your practice safely. Here is some advice on how to do so (Wilson, 2019):

- Dilute all oils in a carrier oil; you can even correspond these to your magickal intentions, so olive would work well here for protection. The percentage of essential oil should not exceed 5% of the total mixture. For reference, six drops to one ounce of carrier oil gives a dilution of 1%.

- Before applying topically, check that the oil is safe to do so, particularly with certain health conditions and medications.
- Like with hair dye, if you mean to apply the oil to yourself or another person, do a patch test first by applying a small amount to the crook of your elbow and observing its effect for 24 hours before washing it off. If there is no reaction, you are good to go.
- Never ingest essential oils or apply them on mucous membranes. They can wreak havoc with your insides.
- Only diffuse oils in a well-ventilated place, and only for around 20–30 minutes at a time.
- Be aware that some oils in the air are harmful to children and pets. Research the safety of your oils before diffusing them.
- Keep out of reach of children and pets.
- Keep away from flames.
- Wash your hands after handling.

Incorporating Moon Phases and Days of the Week Into Your Spells

One way to give your magickal workings an extra bit of "oomph" is by casting spells during specific times. The moon has a powerful effect on magick, and days of the week are ruled by different planets, meaning you can draw on this celestial energy to add extra power to your spiritual endeavors. While sometimes you may need to work a spell right now, there are other times that you can plan ahead, meaning you can tie your work to specific times to make it that much more powerful.

Moon Phases

The moon has a strong relationship to magick and intuition. It has a remarkable effect on our planet, being responsible for tides, and as it ebbs and flows, so do its effects on our magickal workings. Different moon phases are optimized for different things in the following ways (Raine, 2012):

- **New moon:** New beginnings and "planting seeds," especially for things you would like to bring to fruition during a lunar cycle.
- **Waxing moon:** Attracting things to yourself, such as love and prosperity.
- **Full moon:** The most powerful time for magick and psychism. A time for celebration—many Wiccans mark the full moon as "esbats"—and important divination and spell work.

- **Waning moon:** Releasing what does not serve you and banishing negativity.

Days of the Week

As well as the moon phase, you can work

with the days of the week. Each day is ruled by one of the traditional astrological planets and thus takes on their characteristics. This means that each day is primed to be better than others for casting spells relating to their reigning planet. Roger Horne (2019) explains it well in his book *Folk Witchcraft:*

Sunday is ruled by the sun and is associated with healing, happiness, and good fortune. Monday is ruled by the moon and is associated with the second sight [ability to see spirits] and divination. Tuesday is ruled by Mars and is associated with defense and victory over enemies. Wednesday is ruled by Mercury and is associated with trade, communication, and travel. Thursday is ruled by Jupiter and associated with prosperity, luck, and favor. Friday is ruled by Venus and is associated with love, friendship, and beauty. Finally, Saturday is ruled by Saturn, associated with curses, the dead, and baneful workings. (p.33)

Color Magick

Colors, too, carry power. Just as each color has its own wavelength scientifically, so each carries its own specific energy corresponding to different magickal intentions. You can thus incorporate colors into your magickal workings according to what you are seeking to gain. Popular ways to do this involve candles or thread, depending on the form of spell you are using. The meanings of each color are as follows (Chamberlain, 2017a; Saint Thomas, 2018; Wiginton, 2018):

- **Red:** Love, passion, lust, courage, defense, conflict, and power.
- **Pink:** Romance, pure/innocent love, friendship, and self-care.
- **Orange:** Creativity, attraction, physical energy, and self-expression.
- **Yellow:** Abundance, self-confidence, communication, academic pursuits, and happiness.
- **Green:** Prosperity, material possessions, money, and fertility.
- **Light blue:** Peace and healing.
- **Dark blue:** Psychic abilities, protection,

and empathy.

- **Purple:** Intuition and psychic ability, deity work, ambition, and power.
- **Black:** Protection and banishing.
- **White:** Cleansing, purity, connection to the divine, and the truth.
- **Gray:** Complexity, balance, and binding.
- **Brown:** The earth, material possessions, the home, and animals.
- **Gold:** The sun, money, prosperity, and careers.
- **Silver:** The moon, intuition, and psychism.

Working With Deities, Spirits, and Ancestors for Protection

Another way you can protect yourself is by enlisting the help of the various incorporeal entities that surround us. Spirits (particularly spirit guides), ancestors, and deities can all have relationships developed with them, after which point you can ask them for aid in protection.

Who to choose? Well, it all depends on your personal predilections. With deities in particular, many people feel the need to select the "right" one for the job. However, all deities have it within their magnificent abilities to offer protection by dint of their power. Even a deity associated with the gentle realm of love, Aphrodite, carried the cult epithet (a bit like a surname for gods) *Areia* in Ancient Greece, meaning "warlike" (*Aphrodite Titles*, n.d.).

What is more important than the domains that the gods rule over is your personal relationship with them, and this is true with spirits and ancestors as well. In Ancient Greece, this relationship to the divine was known as *kharis*, which can be translated as "grace" or "thankfulness." It describes the relationship of reciprocity between worshipped and worshipper, in which thanks is given for divine assistance and offerings are made even without the expectation of something in return— although when asking for something in particular, it is also considered "best practice" to accompany it with an offering, too (*Kharis (Χάρις) Our Relationship With the Godss*, 2012; Burkert, 1987).

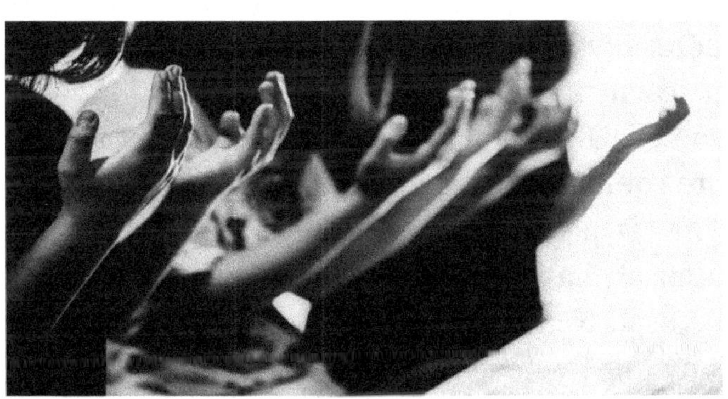

There is also a belief floating around in popular witchcraft circles that states that you need to be "chosen" by a deity to work with them. To put it bluntly, this is false. While sometimes deities do reach out to practitioners, it is just as valid to be interested in one yourself and initiate the relationship.

So, how do we develop these relationships? It is a similar process for all entities, whether deities, ancestors, or spirit guides, and you needn't possess any of the psychic clair senses in order to be able to do so. Like relationships with other humans, communication is key, as is taking care of their needs. This is quite safe, particularly in the case of most deities and ancestors, despite what some may say in different corners of the internet. After all, in the ancient world, even children would join in celebrations and worship of gods.

With respect to communication, this naturally includes prayer—which looks different to each practitioner—but also divination. You can use any divinatory tool to ask the entity you are contacting to give you answers to questions. This is a great way of checking to see if an offering has been received well, but it can also be used to ask for guidance and advice. This is why most witches devote some time to trying to get accustomed to at least one form of divination because it comes in handy for so many things.

Offerings can take place anywhere, such as in nature, but tend to be made on a shrine dedicated to the entity you are giving them to. Pretty much anything can be an offering, even down to a simple glass of water, so it needn't be pricey at all. Many people will offer the first bite of their meal to entities, too, which you can remove a bitesize portion and place upon the shrine. Other popular offerings include plants sacred to that deity, milk, alcohol, coffee, bread, grains, and honey. Many people will also burn incense in the entities' honor. These perishable offerings can be respectfully disposed of when you feel it is right—many people will "return them to the earth" by burying or leaving them outside—but it is also possible to give gifts that will remain on the shrine permanently, such as crystals, shells, plants, and statues. These are known as "votive offerings" (*Offerings to Gods and Ancestors: Paganism Basics,* 2018; Virginia, 2019; Wigington, 2019a, 2020).

By building a regular practice that involves communication and offerings, you will build up a relationship with your entity of choice. Once this has been done, you can call on them, much like how a friend may call on another friend for a favor. When doing so, be sure to accompany the petition with an offering as a sign of good faith. However, if you need to pray quickly on the fly for assistance, you can mention the good standing relationship you have to persuade the entity for help and provide an offering later when you have the time. You should also typically offer again in thanks once the job is done.

HIGH PRIESTESS

CHAPTER 4
BUILDING YOUR MAGICKAL SHIELD

Your spirit is the true shield. – Morihei Ueshiba

Now that you are more aware of the background of magickal protection as well as the basic constituent parts of magick, we can begin to delve into more detail about how to convert this theory into practice. Let's start with the most basic elements: prayer and building a shield. Both are forms of proactive prevention, meaning they will be there for you before an attack happens. There are many ways you can build shields, in particular, but they typically use the power of visualization and what is called "energy work." I'll explain this in more detail below, as well as ways to cleanse your energy and recoup any that is lost by connecting to the earth and the cosmos. Firstly, however, I'll explain why protecting yourself before attacks is a prudent thing to do.

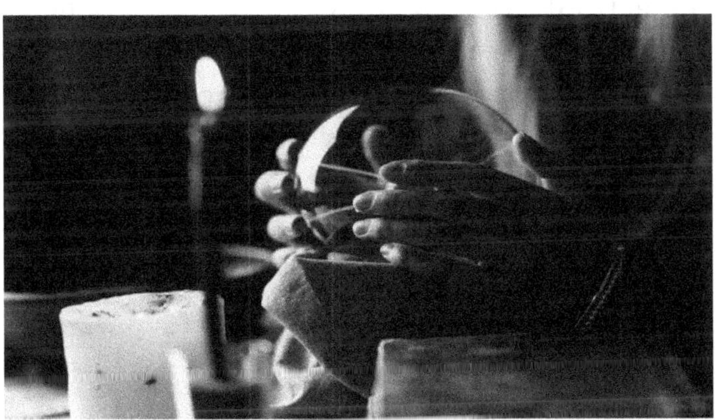

The Importance of Proactive Prevention

Defending yourself when an attack happens is all well and good, but it immediately places you on the back foot. Chances are you're already beset with symptoms—which is how you know you are being attacked—and you need to act quickly to discern the cause and disarm it.

Surely, then, it makes sense to have something in place before an attack of some kind happens. After all, countries don't stand down their armies in the absence of war: They keep them and continue to train them so that they are both a deterrent to those who would wish a nation harm as well as to ensure they are prepared should someone attempt to attack the country.

Magical defense works in much the same way. We put wards in place and shield ourselves energetically to prevent harm from being done to us. They will disarm attacks before they can take place. While no ward or method of shielding is perfect—meaning there will inevitably be ways around it—they can be powerful at preventing a magickal attack from taking root.

Defending Against Psychic Attacks and Witchcraft: Harnessing Your Inner Power and Intuition for Defense

Now that you know the importance of protecting yourself from magickal attack, you're probably now wondering how you go about doing this. One way is to create wards and protective amulets. These will be the focus of the next chapter. What I want to talk about here, however, is something you can tap into at any point: shielding. This combines grounding, visualization, and directed intention—three of the most important basic skills in witchcraft—to work with your own energy reserves. Because the techniques involved are so fundamental to spell casting, it is worth covering them here, as this will then be built on in subsequent chapters when it comes to casting more advanced (but still beginner-friendly) spells.

Shielding

So, what is shielding? It is exactly what it sounds like: the erection of a magickal shield of energy around yourself that prevents external influences from coming in and interfering. Think of science fiction films and television shows like Star Trek: They all talk about shields on spaceships that prevent missiles from landing.

They take the damage of these attacks and keep the actual vessel itself from coming to harm. Magickal shields work in much the same way.

The basic way of shielding can be done on the fly, whenever you want negative energy to run off you like water off a duck's back. All you need is a moment or two to devote to putting your shield in place. When you first begin, it may take a little bit longer to be able to do this, but over time, it will become second nature.

The directions to shield are as follows:

1. Bring your attention to your breath. If it helps, place a hand gently on your tummy to feel the inhales and exhales. Take a moment 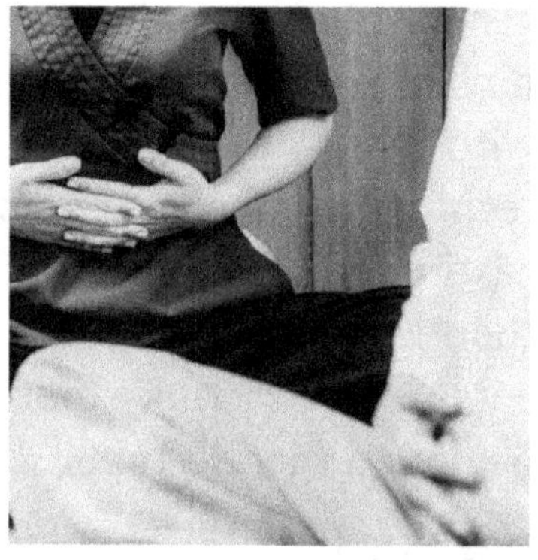 to really concentrate on this. Clear the mind as best as possible. If unwanted thoughts intrude, acknowledge them by saying to yourself, "Thinking," and then, gently redirect attention back onto the breath.

2. Feel the ground under your feet. Feel your

weight pressing down upon it, and the solidity that supports you always. Picture, in your mind, deep roots coming from your feet into the ground. The earth is a constant reservoir of energy: Feel yourself drawing this up through your rooted feet. You may picture this as white light, pure and malleable for your intention.

3. Now, picture outer space above you. Celestial energy—whether that's from the moon, the sun, planets, or the stars—has an indelible effect on us. Feel yourself drawing this energy down through the crown of your head.

4. Sit with this combination for a moment, feeling yourself pulling energy from the earth and the cosmos in tandem. It will land in the center of your body, right behind your solar plexus. This is one method in the practice we call "grounding."

5. Next, when you are ready, "push out" this energy so that it forms a sphere of white light around you. Hold this feeling while thinking your intention clearly: You are protected from magickal attack and negative influence. You may choose to chant something to this effect, such as

As above, so below,
I am protected through this flow.

Shielding me, sheltering me,
From negative influence, I am free.

6. Once you feel adequately protected, you may cease the visualization, knowing that the shield will remain in place. "Top it up" throughout the day if you feel it is necessary. Over time, you will find it easier to sense this energy by using your intuition pretty much reflexively. However, while you are building this skill, you may wish to pause for a moment to focus on the breath again to then "feel out" what your energy feels like and if the shield is still working optimally.

Prayers For Protection: Drawing on Deities and Your Ancestors

Prayer is one way that we commune with deities and sometimes ancestors by speaking our wishes either aloud or internally to them. Because of this, they can be done at any time, in any place. While it is customary to provide an offering with a prayer, if you are out and about, you can do this step later.

Many people worry about saying the wrong thing when praying, but essentially, all you need to do is speak from the heart. So long as what you are saying corresponds with your intentions and is said in an appropriately respectful way, the exact wording of your prayer does not matter. This means you can do it whenever you want, as opposed to only when you have written materials to hand to refer to.

While many people also enjoy writing their prayers to create something more formal, that nevertheless uses their own wording, there is nothing wrong with using a prayer written by someone else. Below are two prayers that I have personally written: one to Mother Nature—called many things within different religions that recognize the divinity of the earth—and another to our ancestors. Feel free to work these prayers into your own magickal practice.

Prayer to Mother Nature

Mother, mother, she who gives,

Upon your face is all that lives,

Ruler over big and small,

Your magnificence is known by all.

I pray today to your holy self,

To ask for protection and good health.

Shield me please from evil and harm,

And bless my mind with total calm.

Look after me and all that I love,

As below and as above.

Prayer to the Ancestors

Ancestors, hear my humble plea:

I thank you for watching over me.

I ask now for your protection.

From all forms of malediction.

Keep me and my loved ones safe and sound,

And to you, there'll be praise all around.

Strengthening Your Aura and Energy Field

Working with energy in this magickal way can be draining. This is one of the reasons that you pull energy from the earth and celestial bodies when doing any form of energy work, like that involved in shielding, as it will help to stop you from being depleted.

If you do feel tired after magick, you should take time to rest. Eating and drinking are also important and will make you feel much better. Additionally, you can reconnect with the earth through your roots and allow any excess energy that may make you feel jittery to drain into it. This is another form of grounding. Over time, you will get better at manipulating your energy as well as that around you and in your tools, meaning magickal burnout of some variety will be much less likely to happen.

Sometimes, our energy can get muddled, though, and it leaves us feeling out of sorts. We just feel a little funky all over or "off," but we can't put a finger on why. Many ancient religions spoke of "pollution" that we pick up in our day-to-day lives. The Ancient Greeks called this miasma, seeing it as something we collect up through human activities such as getting physically dirty, having been around excesses of emotion, having sex, and also experiencing times such as sickness and death as well as birth. Before the Greeks would pray or enter a temple, they would cleanse themselves with their equivalent of holy water, making themselves pure before the gods (Purification in Hellenismos, 2013).

Knowing this about the idea of pollution makes this "off" feeling make sense. We're carrying around energetic baggage from our daily lives, and it lingers about, sapping us of energy and alertness, as well as possibly making any magickal activity less successful because you can't direct a pureness of energy into your spells quite so easily. This is why I used the word "muddled" before because it is kind of like everything is a bit mixed up, and so, you're being pulled in multiple directions at once, rather than being able to focus and live through your intentions.

Cleansing

Fortunately, there are ways to get rid of these negative or polluting influences. Enter cleansing,

sometimes called purification: This is the magickal process by which you give something a spiritual deep-clean, getting rid of what you do not need and reviving that which you do. This is something you can do to yourself, your space, and objects—particularly those that are second-hand, as they are more likely to carry traces of other people's energy.

There are many methods you can use to cleanse something. With all of these, you should make sure to cover the entire space, whether that's around your body, the room, the house, or around the object. Do not neglect nooks, crannies, or corners. Some methods of cleansing include the following (Sebastiani, 2018):

- Using incense: This can take the form of a smoke cleansing bundle—often erroneously called "smudge sticks"—censing with herbs burned (safely!) on charcoal, or with stick incense that can be found cheaply in many locations both online and in the flesh. Make sure the smoke actually touches whatever it is cleansing.
- Sprinkling holy water: This is usually prayed over to bless and consecrate it to the task and is typically composed of water with some sea salt added. You may also add cleansing herbs to it.
- Washing and cleaning: When it comes to yourself, this means a salt scrub in the shower infused with cleansing herb essences or a bath filled with some salt and purifying herbs—or a pre-made infusion of these if you don't want to be picking bits of

herb out of the tub afterward! For spaces and objects, this means giving everything a clean. You can wash floors, walls, and water-safe knickknacks using an infusion of cleansing herbs and use a broom to sweep up—extra points if it is a traditional witch's besom, which looks exactly like the sort of brooms fairytale witches fly upon.

- Sprinkling a specially made cleansing powder: This is made up of pulverized herbs corresponding to these cleansing intentions. Sprinkle them all over, and then, sweep or vacuum it up before emptying the contents outside of the property; after all, if you're trying to rid yourself of something, you don't want it sticking around in the bin!

- Using sound: You may ring a bell, chant, or stomp your feet and clap your hands. When doing the latter, you may also shout out commands for the energy to leave. This more noisy method is particularly effective as the stage you would take before banishing a spirit and after asking it to leave politely.

- The use of fire and light: This would mean safely carrying a candle around and shining its light upon every part of the thing you wish to cleanse.

Many people work cleansing into a schedule of sorts, using the beginnings-related energy of the new moon to cleanse and purify their spaces, and it is also common to cleanse the self before any ritual, offerings, or spell work. On top of this, many witches also habitually revive their wards at certain times, too. These wards are the subject of the next chapter.

CHAPTER 5
THE FIRST LINE OF DEFENSE: PROTECTION MAGICK

Self-defense is not just a set of techniques, it's a state of mind that begins with the belief that you are worth defending. – Rorion Gracie

You've now been equipped with some of the basics of witchcraft, as well as the knowledge of protective herbs and crystals. You've also been able to begin practicing magick through the construction of a shield and methods of cleansing. This is a good foundation for what comes next: proactive protection magick. In this chapter, I'll walk you through how to come up with what sort of protection you'd like to construct, before giving you some ready-made spells that you can cast whenever the fancy takes you. However, at the end of the

chapter, I'll cover how to write your own spells, meaning you can also take those listed here as inspiration and alter them to better fit your purposes—as well as what materials you have at hand. This chapter, then, will serve as a strong foundational practice of witchcraft aimed at protecting you from magickal or psychic attack.

Creating a Personal Protection Plan

I have previously spoken about layering up your protections. Rather than scattering your energy in one spell that attempts to do too many things at once—in which the blowback is harder to predict because of the vagueness of the intentions—it is better to put some time into multiple, more targeted spells. While this requires some planning, the energy used shouldn't differ too much from one big, far-reaching spell that would require massive amounts to actually achieve its aims.

So, what sort of spells should you do? That all depends on what you want to protect. As a minimum, I would recommend warding yourself and your property against harm. You may break this down further into wards specifically targeting certain things, such as protection from spirits and protection from theft. This means you can tinker and tailor your approach to all your different needs. You can also use what you learned in the previous chapter about shielding and cleansing to combine with wards and create a comprehensive plan of protection.

Magick, however, will never last forever. It requires energy and to be refreshed. Many witches use the lunar cycle as a marker of when they cleanse and ward, such as every new moon. This doesn't necessarily look like starting from scratch, depending on what methods you have chosen, but may look like "feeding" energy to your already existing wards by completely burning an enchanted candle in their presence.

When it comes to planning when to cleanse and shield yourself, you will need to factor in your own circumstances. Someone who works in a customer-facing role will be more likely to need to do this more often than someone who works from home. Natural empaths—which you'll remember are people who can feel the emotions of others without being told about them—also tend to need to do this more regularly, as I have already stated.

It is worth, then, thinking about your own circumstances before deciding what your personal protection plan should look like. Research the different types of spells—using those contained within this book as inspiration—to see what will work best for you.

For instance, if you need to be discreet about your craft, a jar spell or another physically enchanted object probably isn't the best choice.

Once you have an idea of what will work for you, write it down somewhere you won't forget

it. Many witches advise the keeping of a grimoire or "book of shadows": a specially crafted journal or document that you populate with all things related to your craft, such as research, experiment notes, and spell logs. If you haven't already started one of these, I would strongly recommend it, as recordkeeping allows you to track your practice as a witch over time. A personal protection plan would fit into this sort of book.

Protective Circles and Barriers

Many witches and other practitioners of magick will "cast a circle" before carrying out magick and rituals. But what is this? Essentially, a circle is a demarcation of spiritual space that both holds energy within it to power a spell while also keeping out unwanted interference (Wigington, 2018b). In a way, it's a bit like the shields we have already discussed, except this time it's about protecting a space. While not every witchcraft practice requires a circle, and sometimes, you need to do a spell on the fly without time to prepare something like this, casting a circle does carry the benefits I have already mentioned, as well as helping you to get into the right frame of mind for magick through the ritual actions. As such, I would recommend casting one when you do have the opportunity to prepare your magickal workings.

Casting a circle is fortunately a very beginner-friendly practice. Each witch will have a different method of doing so, some more elaborate than others, and some that call on the guardians of the elements. Here is mine, which you'll find is quite simple. To cast this circle, you will need a wand or athame. In a pinch, you can use the index finger on your dominant, projecting hand.

The directions are as follows (Alexander, 2014):

1. Have your workspace all ready to go, making sure you have all the tools and ingredients necessary to complete your spell.
2. Ground and center yourself using the

methods already outlined in this book, pulling energy from the earth and the celestial sphere.

3. Holding your wand or athame or pointing out your finger if you do not have these, face west. Visualizing your energy pouring forth from your finger, slowly turn clockwise and see it drawing a sphere all the way around you, until you face the same direction again.

If at any point you need to leave the circle, use the wand, athame, or your finger to cut a doorway out of it, making sure to close it behind you. When you return, you will need to do the same thing again.

Dismantling a circle after your spell work or ritual is done involves the same steps as casting one, except instead of turning clockwise (sometimes known as "deosil"), you turn counter-clockwise (sometimes known as "widdershins") and imagine the energy falling away. This is because moving clockwise in magic is used to invoke, while counter-clockwise is for banishment.

Evoking Deities, Guardian Spirits, and Guides for Protection

There is some confusion in the witchcraft

community about the difference between "invoking" and "evoking" gods, spirits, ancestors, and guides. Often, these terms are erroneously used interchangeably. However, there is a difference between these. To invoke an entity is to offer oneself up as a vessel for their power so that they appear in this realm through you. As such, it is more akin to a form of consensual possession. Evoking, on the other hand, is an invitation for the entity to join your ritual or spell work, usually to lend their power to you in an external way (Wigington, 2017).

So, how do you go about evoking a deity or guide of sorts for protection while conducting magick or to protect you in general? In fact, I have already covered this in Chapter 3. Evoking involves the same sort of communication that you would usually use for entities. To evoke one is to ask them to attend a ritual and lend their power to it whilst providing them with an offering for them to do so. This would be done after you have created your magickal circle but before you commence the spell work itself.

Once done, you will likely feel a shift in the energy of the circle, if this is something you are attuned to, or perhaps a sensation in your body of something else being there. If you can't feel anything, don't worry: Perceiving energetic changes around you and the presence of entities is a form of psychism, and it develops as a skill over time.

Once you have finished your spell work, you would thank whoever you have evoked for attending before you dismantle your circle. You may then make an offering later, at the time the spell has had its desired effect.

As said in Chapter 3, entities such as deities, ancestors, and spirit guides can also be evoked on the fly if you feel you need protection. Simply say a prayer—either out loud or in your head—asking for help, potentially referencing how good your relationship with the entity is, and then make an offering later when you have the ability to do so.

Warding Your Home, Workplace, and Personal Space

Now that I have covered how to prepare a sacred space for your spell work that will also help to raise and contain energy while keeping out external influence you'd rather not engage with, we can come to the exciting bit: "proper" spells!

Below are a selection of protection spells from my personal grimoire. These are aimed at creating wards for your property. We'll start with sigils because these are a magickal technique that can be applied in a variety of ways to create powerful spells that require less effort and fewer ingredients. I'll then go through some spells that can be used for your house and your car—two pieces of property that people like to enchant with a protective energy. These spells, however, can be adapted to be used for other items of value to yourself; at the end of this chapter, I'll go through how to write your own spells, which will allow you to alter anything I have written for different purposes.

Making Sigils for Multiple Uses

Sigil comes from the Latin *"sigillum"* meaning "seal," but in occult spaces, it refers to a symbol created for magickal purposes

(Merriam-Webster, n.d.-b). In this sense, we can say that we take our energy and intent and seal it into a magickal device of sorts that allows us to utilize that power whenever we draw the sigil onto something.

Originally taken as a concept from ceremonial magick, the modern-day usage of sigils comes from the work of chaos magicians, such as Peter J Carrol (Woodfield, 2022). However, one needn't follow this particular tradition to practice sigil magick. Popularity has exploded in recent years for this method, and you can see why: By magickally forging a symbol that carries such power, we can use it as and when required to quickly cast a spell. This is an incredibly handy technique to have in your repertoire!

So, how do you make a sigil? Kerry Woodfield (2022) gives a comprehensive overview of the various techniques to do this in her book *Sigil Magick,* but I will condense the steps here and combine them with my own personal method of making a

sigil. The steps are as follows, and you will need a pen, paper, a cauldron (or other heatproof dish), and either a lighter or matches:

1. Prepare your sacred space, as well as yourself, by grounding and centering your mind on the task at hand. This may involve some level of meditation and breathwork to activate a more magickal state of mind.

2. Think about how to word your intent as concisely as possible but only in terms of positives. Don't use negative words. So, instead of saying, "Do not let harm come to me," you would say, "Protect me."

3. Write out your intent on a piece of paper. Cross out all the vowels and any repeating letters. This is the first level of abstraction, as sigil magick is dependent on the end result not being legible as a word or phrase.

4. Now is the fun part! Play with the shapes of the remaining letters to create a design. It needn't be ornate or a piece of award-winning art: So long as there is a level of abstraction between the symbol and what it is supposed to represent, it will work.

5. Next, it is time to charge your sigil. Place your dominant hand on top of the

completed mark—this is the hand that projects energy. Now, ground yourself as you have already learned, pulling energy from the earth and the celestial realm. Focus your mind entirely on your intent. Visualize, in detail, using all the senses if possible, what that intent looks like when it is enacted.

6. Once the energy has built to a point that you can no longer hold anymore, see it flowing from you into the sigil. You will know when you have emptied the energy into it.

7. Make a copy of the sigil if you intend to use it regularly so that you will not forget it. Your grimoire/book of shadows would work well as a reliquary for these.

8. Fold the piece of paper that you have charged towards you—this is how to invoke; folding away from the body is used to banish). Light it on fire, and then place it in a heatproof dish to burn out completely. Sprinkle the ashes onto the earth outside or into a plant pot if you do not have access to a green space.

There is debate about whether or not one should look at a sigil after it has been made. Some say it should be forgotten consciously so that the subconscious mind can power it. Others say this does not matter at all and like to reuse sigils. I am of the latter camp, personally. So long as the sigil has been charged and released into the world upon its creation, it can be harnessed with further intent and energy to be used multiple times. Indeed, it is worth me giving some examples of places where you may put a sigil of protection:

- drawn onto the bottom of your shoe
- sewn into the inside lining of a coat or jacket
- on a piece of paper folded up and placed in your purse or wallet
- drawn using consecrated water—salt water prayed over to bless it with the holiness of the self or of a deity—onto walls, windows, or doors
- drawn onto the inside of a car's glove box
- doodled onto the arm
- drawn on the face when applying makeup and then blended out for subtlety
- drawn on the self using moisturizer and then rubbed into the body
- stirred into your morning coffee or other hot drink to be ingested
- traced in the air using incense

As you can see, there are some temporary

and some permanent methods of using a sigil here. Naturally, those that are temporary will need to be recharged with intent and energy more regularly as it is always good to refresh your wards. However, just because it is drawn and then disappears does not diminish the strength of the sigil. One of the benefits of this method is that it can be used in so many ways. I'm sure that, with practice, you will come up with some of your own.

Jar Spell for Home Protection

Jar spells are all over social media at the moment and draw on the long tradition of the witch bottles that I covered in Chapter 1. This particular jar spell is designed to protect your home from being invaded by negativity in any form and send the negative energy back to where it came from. If you would prefer it to simply protect, rather than bite back, you can remove the nails. Do also ensure that the herbs you use are dried: Any moisture content will cause the jar to grow mold. If it still grows mold, you can then know that it has likely caught harm coming towards the home, and therefore, the ward needs to be replaced.

Time

Perform this during the waxing moon on a Tuesday to draw on the power of bringing protection towards you.

Ingredients

- A red candle and something to inscribe it, such as your athame
- A protective incense such as frankincense
- A small glass jar
- Seven nails, preferably iron (iron is associated with protection, and the number seven is particularly magickal)
- Salt (associated with nullifying magick and cleansing)
- Vervain
- Chamomile
- Basil
- Garlic
- Rosemary
- A piece of obsidian that can fit into the jar

- A piece of red jasper that can also fit in the jar

Directions

1. Prepare for the spell work in the usual way.
2. Light the incense.
3. Inscribe the candle with a protective sigil or simply the word "protection" before lighting it.
4. Pass the glass jar through the incense smoke saying

   With the smoke, I cleanse and charge,
   By my will, you will protect this home.

5. Begin to fill the jar. With each ingredient, pour your personal energy and intention into it. Each time, pass the items through the incense smoke as you instruct them of their role. Any words will do, but make sure they relate to the item's correspondences and purpose. For instance, with the basil, say you are drawing on it to protect the home, whereas with the nails, you would say they both protect and return the harm back to whence it came.
6. Once the jar is filled, seal it with the candle wax.

Warding Powder

As I showed in the last chapter, powders can be useful for cleansing. However, they can also be used for warding. This powder is constructed in advance to be used not just immediately but in the future, too. This means it is easy to refresh, as you will simply need to re-sprinkle it.

Time

Make this during the waning moon on a Tuesday to draw on the power of banishing harm. Sprinkle it at regular intervals, such as on the first Tuesday of each waning moon.

Ingredients

- Rosemary
- Nettle
- Onion powder
- Garlic powder
- Pepper
- Bay leaf

Make sure to really grind up the ingredients by using a mortar and pestle so that the warding powder is as fine as you can make it. As you do so, instruct it on its role, perhaps chanting the words "protect and banish." Use the energy generated by the grinding motion to charge the powder.

Once made, this can then be sprinkled around the perimeter of your property. However, if you cannot encircle your property, sprinkling it around the entrances to your home will suffice.

Protection Charm for the Car

Many people worry about their cars and journeys within them and so choose to create a special protection charm for them. This spell works in the same way as the jar spell: through depositing the enchanted ingredients, first passed through incense, into the bag. This spell, however, has two differences: Firstly, you needn't use a candle as you won't be sealing the bag in this way. Secondly, you will knot the bag three times to close it up once the spell is done because the number three is another witchy, magickal number. Once created, you can either hang the pouch from your rear mirror or store it away in your glove box for something more subtle.

Time

Create these protection charms on a Wednesday, which is associated with travel, and during a waxing moon.

Ingredients

- A small red pouch
- A small piece of lapis lazuli
- A small piece of tiger's eye
- A cinnamon stick
- A bay leaf

Amulets for Protection of the Self

Now that I have covered how to ward property, I can move on to my spell that revolves around protecting the self. When it comes to this, it can be better to have something that relates to you specifically because it carries your energy. This is why this particular spell uses a piece of jewelry that you already have. Because it is meaningful to you, it has a strong tie that can be manipulated by magick to protect you. The spell itself can be adapted with ease for a variety of circumstances: general protection, protection from the evil eye—using a nazar here would be doubly useful—or protection during travel. This spell, then, takes an everyday object and consecrates it to be worn daily.

Time

Imbue your amulet with magick on a Tuesday during the waxing moon.

Ingredients

- A bowl (perhaps your cauldron) of salt water
- Your chosen piece of jewelry
- Protective incense such as frankincense
- A red candle and your athame to inscribe it with

Directions

1. Prepare for the spell as you usually would.
2. Light the incense.
3. Inscribe the candle with a protective sigil or the word "protection," and light it.
4. Pass the jewelry through the smoke of the incense, saying, "By power of air, I enchant you to protect."
5. Pass the jewelry over the flame of the

candle (without touching it), saying, "By power of flame, I enchant you to protect."

6. Sprinkle the jewelry with the salt water, saying, "By power of earth and water, I enchant you to protect."

7. Hold the jewelry in your hands, and fill it with your own energy and intent, clearly visualizing in positive terms what you would like it to do.

8. Conclude the spell as you usually would.

Designing Your Own Protection Spells and Charms

The amount of spells that you can do for protection is limited only by your imagination and access to resources. The latter will accumulate over time as you build up the physical arsenal of your magickal workings, and you needn't rush out to buy everything straight away, as I have already said.

The former, however, can be difficult to tap into, especially when you're first starting out with magick. There is a way you can build your imagination, however: building your knowledge. Witchcraft isn't always the glamorous casting of spells, you see. It involves dedication, and some of that needs to be around educating yourself about magick. The fact that you've picked up this book and gotten this far is a sign that you're committed. However, one source is never enough. I encourage you to go out and research any of the concepts in this book further; the references section at the end will be able to direct you to the sources I have drawn from throughout. By educating yourself in this way, you will be able to start building your own spells.

So, what does the spell-writing process look like? You might break it down into stages as follows:

1. **Decide what the spell is for**: This would mean thinking about your intent and what you want to achieve. It is best to be as specific here as possible so that your energy is not scattered.
2. **Decide the method of the spell:** Do you want to make a jar or sachet? How about an amulet? Or perhaps, you need a quick candle spell for a one-off event you're trying to bring about or prevent? Consider your intention and what form of spell would best suit it.
3. **Choose your ingredients:** Refer to

correspondence lists to find ingredients that match your intention. You might also look into the folklore surrounding certain objects, the psychology of color, or even the medicinal qualities of certain herbs. If you're trying to cast a spell that helps with nightmares, for instance, a herb that assuages anxiety and aids sleep, such as valerian, may come in useful.

4. **Choose your timing:** Refer to the moon phases and days of the week in Chapter 3, and choose the best time for your spell. This will give it an added celestial boost.

5. **Plan the steps:** Once you know everything you need to complete the spell, the method you're using, and why you're actually doing it, you can begin to plot out the steps. It is best practice to write these steps down to refer back to later, and so, they should be put in your grimoire or book of shadows. Make sure that your explanation is easy to follow and every step makes sense. Consider writing your own spoken words to accompany certain actions, for words have power and help us to focus our intent and energy on the spell. They needn't rhyme, although sometimes it

feels more magickal for them to do so.

Once you have completed the spell, make a dated record of how it went and if you made any changes while actually doing it. Later, record the outcome of the spell: Did it work? How? Were there any unforeseen consequences? By keeping records of your magickal workings, you can chart your progress over time.

Ideas That You Can Build a Spell Around

It would be remiss of me to leave you here without a little more guidance. Instead of fleshing out more spells for you, I want to give you the opportunity to come up with your own based on some prompts. These little kernels of magick can be taken and have a more formal spell written around them—one as complicated or simple as you wish it to be.

These ideas come from folk magick and knowledge or correspondences. You will develop quite the collection of nuggets of information about these things as you progress in your research into witchcraft. For now, however, here are those that I have picked out for you to experiment with (King, 2016; Pennick, 2021):

- Tie a naturally "holey stone" to your keys to guard your home; holey stones are pebbles with naturally occurring holes, and they are thought to be protective.
- Hang a horseshoe above your front door—upwards to attract luck or downwards to protect from evil.
- Draw sigils on the bottoms of your shoes to protect you when you go out walking.
- Plant a protective herb either outdoors or in a pot for indoor display (checking which is appropriate for your chosen flora), and tend to it, giving it instructions to protect the home.
- Create a poppet (usually incorrectly called "voodoo dolls") to represent someone, and fill it with protective herbs and crystals.
- Make a witch's ladder—a string with feathers and other charms tied onto it at

intervals—to be hung in the home for protection.

- Create a wash for the home out of herbs or essential oils (remembering the safety tips from Chapter 3) to wash down windows and doors with.
- Craft an enchanted oil that can be used to anoint people and objects.
- Using your favorite method of art, create something that you pour your creative energy into to use as a ward, such as a painting, a clay ornament, or a knitted blanket—great for protecting children from nightmares.

Anoint a candle, carve a sigil upon it, and allow it to burn down completely.

CHAPTER 6
REACTIVE MAGICK

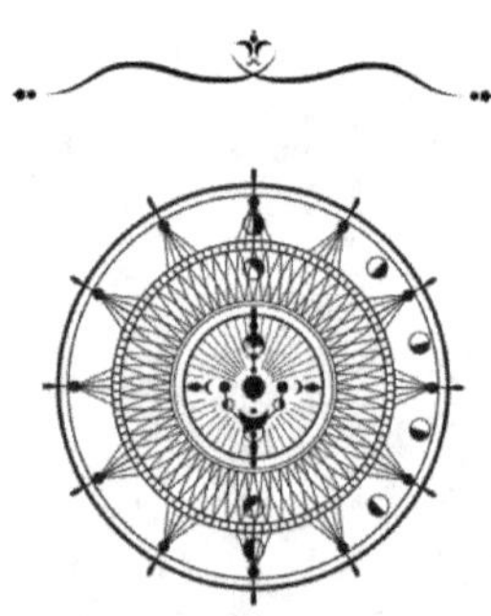

Remember, your words can plant gardens or burn whole forests down. – Gemma Troy

With proactive protection in place, you're covered from a wide variety of harms. However, sometimes, things still slip through the net and catch us unawares. That's why it pays to know how to perform reactive magick before you need to do it because, then, you're prepared for any eventuality.

What do I mean by reactive magick? This is essentially any spell that is used in reaction to harm and includes things like hex-breaking and banishing. You may also wish to give a bit of a kick up the butt to the person sending negative energy your way. In this case, you will likely be interested in a return-to-sender spell. It's not up to me to tell you the rights or wrongs of this action: Your ethics are your own business, and as we covered in Chapter 1, different people will view these things differently. However, it would be remiss of me to not include this in case you are of a mind that you would like to do a spell such as this.

Therefore, this chapter is a compendium of tactics on how to respond to magickal or psychic harm. Follow on as I walk you through how to deal with hexes and how to banish negative influences in your space.

Uncrossing and Hex-Breaking Spells

You may come across a variety of terms to describe spells that remove curses and hexes as well as psychic attacks. In this section, I will go through what an "uncrossing" spell is while paying attention to the difficult issue that is cultural appropriation, something that I covered briefly in the introduction when talking about traditions involving initiation. I will then give you a template spell for hex-breaking. While this spell will work on its own if followed correctly, you can also adapt it for your own uses, potentially making it more specific to your needs or substituting ingredients you do not have by using the correspondence list in Chapter 3. This section, then, will go through all you need to know about how to remove curses in a way that does not send them back to wherever they came from, as that is the focus of the section that follows.

Uncrossing Spells and Cultural Appropriation

In a thesis written by Kathryn Gottlieb (2017), a definition of cultural appropriation is given:

Cultural appropriation suggests a number of things: that the person doing the appropriating is in some way more powerful than the group they are appropriating from (for example, a white person who is inherently privileged in most of Western society); that the appropriation is done without the consent of the group that is being appropriated from (if an individual is given a piece of cultural material as a gift, it is not generally seen as cultural appropriation); and that the appropriation in some way does harm to the group that is being appropriated from (for example, if the appropriation perpetuates stereotypes). (p. 4)

It is also often defined as one group benefitting from another. For example, if someone manages to make money off of a culture that is not their own, they are appropriating. The same can be said of gaining social acclaim for one's appropriation, particularly when people from the culture in question often receive negativity for taking part in their heritage.

How does this apply to uncrossing spells? A quick Google search shows many oils used for such magick for sale. On one website, however, it is pointed out that such spells come from African diasporic practices such as Hoodoo (Uncrossing: Removing Negative Energy 2021).

As I have already covered, these practices are considered closed to outsiders. This is because of a complex interplay of factors. Hoodoo and other such diasporic practices come from the spirituality of enslaved peoples who tried to keep alive the spirit of the religions they followed on their home continent while adapting to a life of  Christianity. As such, they are syncretic between these religions and, most importantly, carry a history of persecution as well as being a constant reminder of the oppression of Black people during this period. Because of this, it is mostly agreed upon that only people of African descent can practice these religions and spiritualities, whether or not this is an initiatory tradition like Haitian Vodou or something more akin to folk magick like Hoodoo.

Because of this, and the fact that I am not Black, I will not be taking it upon myself to share an uncrossing ritual, as it goes against my personal values of respecting the cultural traditions of other people in the ways that they have requested. If you are desperate to know more, there are a plethora of resources about this online. However, as with all ethical issues within witchcraft—of which there are many, as you have seen—I encourage you to think carefully about whether or not it is appropriate for you to take this type of spell work into your own spiritual practice.

A Method for Hex-Breaking

There are, nevertheless, many ways you can break a hex, and fortunately, they are accessible for those unfamiliar with such magick. You already know of one: The egg cleanse and divination covered in Chapter 2 can work to remove curses if they are present. In this case, you would cleanse until the yolk is no longer showing signs of a curse being present (such as breaking).

However, if you're looking for something else to do, there is one spell I have created that uses a poppet, which as I have already said is often erroneously called a "voodoo doll." While poppets are used by some rootworkers, they also appear in many folk magick practices across the globe and are therefore an open method that we can use to divert the curse or hex and then eventually break it entirely.

Time

If it is possible to wait, hex-breaking will be most effective on the night of the new moon.

Ingredients

- Black cotton, thread, and a needle to sew
- A taglock associated with you, such as hair or nail clippings
- Frankincense incense
- Thistle
- A bay leaf
- A black pen
- Chili
- Nettle
- Vervain

Directions

1. Prepare for the ritual in your usual way.
2. Light the incense.

3. Begin to construct a basic poppet. Cut two pieces out of the cotton in a shape that resembles a human. Sew mostly together, leaving a gap through which you can stuff it.

4. Pass all the herbs apart from the bay leaf through incense while instructing them of their purpose to break the hex placed against you, and stuff these herbs inside the poppet.

5. Write the words "free from curses" on the bay leaf, pass it through the incense smoke, and place it inside the poppet.

6. Pass the taglock through the incense smoke, and place it inside the poppet, saying

> *With part of me, you become my copy,*
> *Do this job, and don't be sloppy!*
> *In my place, you take this curse,*
> *Back to my usual state I will reverse.*
> *Across this moon, you work for me,*
> *At the next new moon, I shall be free.*

7. Sew up the poppet.

8. Hold the poppet in your hands, and say

> *With my breath, I give you life,*
> *You will free me from this strife.*

9. Breathe across the poppet. It is now

activated, so to speak. You can now place it away somewhere hidden but which you will nevertheless not forget.

10. At the next new moon, dispose of the poppet somewhere away from your property. If you can, bury it beneath the earth, but otherwise, ensure you get rid of it entirely.

Return-to-Sender Spells

Sometimes, we don't want to play nice. Sometimes, someone or something will only be deterred from harming you if you bite back. Maybe, you're just royally peeved by their behavior and think they need to learn a lesson. In these instances, you may decide to opt for a return-to-sender spell. As well as breaking a curse or magickal attack, these spells will also turn the harm caused back onto whoever is sending it your way. It is a cost-effective (in terms of energy expended) way of both nullifying an attack against you and hexing someone in return: Instead of doing two separate spells, you can do just one and it will be done.

Spiky Shields

Also relevant to this section is the notion of adapting the shields you learned to construct in Chapter 4 to also redirect negative energy back to where it came from. I'll cover this first as it is the most simple of the techniques covered here. I call these protections "spiky shields" partly because of the visualization of them but also because they remind me of a cactus. Cacti protect themselves from predators by growing spikes that will prick and hurt those who attempt to harm them. Spiky shields work in much the same way: They will prick back at any negativity that comes towards you.

The process of creating a spiky shield is quite simple. You would begin the visualization exercise to construct a shield that was covered in Chapter 4. However, when it comes to holding a picture of the shield in your head, you would see spikes sticking out of it. Perhaps, this looks like a cactus, if we use my previous examples, or like thorny vines writhing around the shield. Imagine negative energy coming towards the shield, getting caught on a spike, and retreating in pain.

Hold this visualization in your head until you feel that the shield has formed around you. At this point, it is done, and it can be refreshed in the same ways discussed in Chapter 4.

A Basic Return-to-Sender Spell Template

Let's get back into the more fun stuff, shall we? Below is a return-to-sender spell from my personal grimoire. By allowing a cord between two candles to burn, you will cut the energetic cord of the curse between yourself and the person involved, while the particular ingredients within the spell will ensure that they feel the spell bounce back onto them. It is important that the candles burn down fully, so select small ones that can be burned in one sitting. There are many small, thin spell candles available to purchase online.

Time

Return-to-sender spells are best cast on a Saturday during the waning moon.

Ingredients

- A small black candle that can be burned in one sitting
- A small red candle that can be burned in one sitting
- Your athame for carving the candles
- Red thread
- A heatproof tray or dish large enough to place both candles in with space between them
- Sea salt
- Chili flakes
- Black pepper
- Cactus spikes, rose thorns, or any other sharp materials from plants
- Nettle

Directions

1. Prepare for the spell in the usual way.
2. Carve the black candle with a sigil of your target's name or, if unknown, something you feel represents them.
3. Carve the red candle with a protective sigil.

4. Melt the bottom of the candles with a lighter, enough to soften a little bit of wax, and use this to stick the candles to the surface of your tray or dish.

5. Circle the candles with sea salt, the herbs, and the spikes or thorns you have selected, pouring your intention into each ingredient and instructing them of their purpose as you do so.

6. Wrap the red thread around the candles seven times to bind them together, securing with three knots.

7. Light the candles and say

> *You've done me harm, and now, it's your turn,*
> *With these candles, our connection I burn,*
> *Once they are gone, it will be returned to you,*
> *And after that, our business is through.*

8. Allow the candles to burn down, including allowing the thread to separate with the flames.

9. Once the spell is done, dispose of the remnants outside away from your property.

10. Cleanse yourself in an appropriate way

once the spell has been fully completed—good practice for any baneful magick.

Unraveling Generational Curses

Let me preface this section by saying that generational curses are very rare. As Avery Hart (2023) says, you'll usually know that you're affected by one because they become part of your family's lore. If you're not sure that a generational curse is to blame for your hardship, do some thorough divination before proceeding as usually what is mistaken for a curse is just bad luck or familial cycles of traumatic norms. Consider even procuring the services of a trusted professional diviner for further information.

Essentially, generational curses are long-standing baneful magick cast upon a family, which are then passed down until someone deals with them. Unfortunately, sometimes that person has to be you as, for whatever, reason your ancestors were unable to do so.

However, your ancestors will be your greatest allies in finally dismantling such baneful magick. They will, by dint of being related to you, be interested in seeing these curses gone. Ancestors are there to guide and protect their descendants, after all, and they have the power to do remarkable things in their new life in death. Remember this for the moment, while I take an aside to discuss what generational curses more often are.

Essentially, it is rare for magick to last beyond a generation. It will usually die when the person who cast it dies. But with generational curses, knowledge of it is passed down between members of the family. Everyone knows about it, no matter how long ago it was, and over time, the curse becomes mythologized but still fervently believed in. As belief is so powerful in magick—indeed, it is often said that the best way to curse someone is to make them think you've cursed them and let their subconscious do all the hard work for you—it becomes a self-perpetuating cycle in which the belief ends up being the fuel for the effects. As such, to break the curse, you need to break the belief. This means performing one hell of a hex-breaking spell, drawing on as much theatrics as possible to thoroughly dismantle belief in the curse because the family members believe in the hex-breaker more than the curse that predated it.

So, essentially, breaking a generational curse is about breaking the belief in it. It's more about psychology than anything else. Write down all your beliefs about the curse on one piece of paper and thoroughly interrogate them. Did your relationship end because of the curse, or did things just turn sour when your partner had a wandering eye—something that happens in 15–20% of marriages (Montemayor, 2023)? Then, you need to work on your psychology over a period of time to believe the rational reasons rather than the mystical ones. Remember the golden rule of witchcraft: Mundane explanations are much more unlikely than magickal ones.

However, if you're still not reassured—and perhaps, your family isn't either—it doesn't hurt to do a curse-breaking ritual. The method for hex-breaking already covered will be of use here, and you may adapt it for your specific circumstances. As I have said, your ancestors will want to help; they take a strong interest in their family line and love to act as guides and guardians, and so, calling upon their aid with the spell will be sure to boost its power.

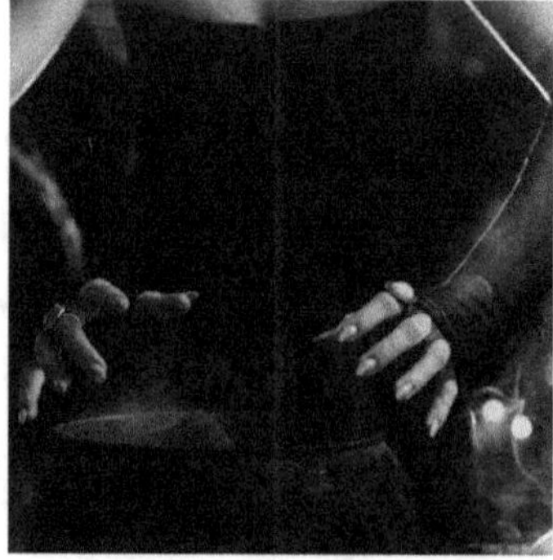

Still struggling? Here is a spell that may help draw on the power of your ancestors. Make sure to again choose a candle small enough to burn in one sitting.

Time

It is most effective to evoke your ancestors on a Tuesday during the waning moon.

Ingredients

- A red candle
- Your athame for carving
- A cauldron with sand in it, for safe burning
- A small stick or twig of oak, ash, or cedar and a marker to write on it
- Olive oil
- Salt water
- Protective incense such as frankincense
- An offering for your ancestors, such as

coffee or alcohol (if they drank)

Directions

1. Cast your circle as you usually would.
2. Place the offering upon your workspace, hold your arms into the air spread apart with your hands open, and say

> *Ancestors of mine, hear my plea:*
> *Tonight, I move to set us free.*
> *With this offering, I call upon you*
> *To help me see this magick through.*
> *Stand by my side, and lend your aid,*
> *And I shall undo what was once made.*

3. Light the protective incense. Cleanse yourself and your ingredients with it, instructing them of their purpose.
4. Anoint the candle with olive oil by rubbing it from bottom to top (avoiding the wick), moving your fingers away from your body—moving away is to banish, while towards is to attract.
5. Carve a sigil on the candle that represents the word "release" to you or, failing that, simply carve that word.
6. Watch the candle as it burns down. Think about all the misfortune of you and your loved ones vanishing and the prosperity and joy that will follow.

7. When the candle is almost entirely burned, grab the stick and write on it "Curse on [your family name]." Hold it in your right hand and say

> *Honored tree, you now serve as a representation,*
> *With my breath, I make this mutation:*
> *You become the curse, and the curse becomes you.*

8. Breathe onto the stick. Snap it in half. Burn both pieces.

9. Once the candle has burned down, dispose of the remnants away from your property—preferably at a crossroads—and scatter the ashes of the stick into the wind away from you. Turn, walk away, and do not look back.

10. Thoroughly cleanse yourself and the space in which you cast the spell. It is done.

When Cleanses Don't Work: The Basics of Banishing

It is rare to have spiritual visitors who are troublesome in some way. While popular ghost-hunting shows would have you believe that poltergeists and demons are always around the corner, ready to torment humanity, in actual fact, this kind of activity is pretty rare. Most spirits and other nonhuman entities are happy to live and let live and will only really interact

with you if you try to work with them—something some witches do, calling it "spirit work."

However, on rare occasions, someone does come and cause ructions. In these circumstances, you should first try to get them to disappear politely. As I have said in previous chapters, you wouldn't immediately start screaming and shouting obscenities at cold callers at your door—or, at least, I hope not! Instead, you can connect with the spirit through divination to find out what they want and see if there's any way you can help them so long as they promise to leave. Otherwise, you can open a window and politely ask them to leave through it. Give your house a thorough cleanse—my favorite method is with smoke cleansing sticks made from cleansing herbs such as rosemary or garden sage—however, not white sage as it is actually endangered and a closed practice to Native Americans. With these methods, your problem will likely be solved.

Still not budging? Up the ante. Cleanse the house again, and use some sound this time too. Stomp your feet, shout at the entity to leave, and warn it that you will take further action should it not heed your words. Remember the essence of the Terry Pratchett quote at the beginning of this book: Witches should remember that they are feared just as much as unwanted spirits, and you do have the skills to remove them. Back up your words with confidence and strong conviction, and your unwanted lodger will probably clear out.

However, in the rarest of circumstances, the presence may remain. In these instances, when cleansing and telling the entity off does not work, you'll need to take action to forcibly banish them. Some witches frown down upon banishing as a form of baneful magick: After all, you are evicting someone with a bit of a kick up the butt. However, you can't live your life if you have someone meddlesome around who is causing trouble and won't go no matter how firmly you state your desires. As such, it is my opinion that allowing the spirit or entity to remain is causing more harm, as you are hurting yourself! Because of this, I see little to no ethical quandaries when it comes to banishing. So long as you don't jump the gun and banish anything and everything—something which would also end up depleting your energy—you should be fine.

An All-Purpose Banishing Ritual

Below is my purpose-built banishing spell, inspired by Thalia Thorne (2020) but with some changes to personalize it to my style. This spell involves creating your own incense cones, which sounds tricky but is actually rather simple. By creating your own incense, you can pour your intentions into the cones so that when they burn, they release your intentions into your space and pack more of a punch than pre-bought cleansing sticks. The ingredients involved are also specific to banishing as well as the addition of a cleansing herb. The use of a crystal allows you to trap the spirit's link to your space and remove it from the property. It's a bit like physically picking them up and hauling them out the door before locking it behind you.

Time

If possible a Tuesday during the waning moon is best, but usually, banishings cannot wait, and you should not put up with annoyance or harm just because you're waiting for the right moon phase.

Ingredients

- A piece of obsidian
- Salt water
- A red candle
- Your athame for carving
- Distilled water
- Basil
- Frankincense
- Lavender
- Rosemary
- A mortar and pestle

Directions

1. Prepare your space and circle as you usually would. Call on any deities, guides, or ancestors you would like the aid of

with an offering.

2. Grind up the herbs in the mortar and pestle while visualizing your intent. Use your rage to power them, telling them what they will do for you.

3. Once the herbs are a fine powder, add a little distilled water to them until they make a paste.

4. Shape the doughy herbs into a cone. Allow it to dry.

5. Once the incense is dried, carve a banishing sigil on the candle. Light it along with your handmade cone.

6. Consecrate the obsidian by passing it through the smoke of the incense, above the flame of the candle, and sprinkling it with salt water, saying something along the lines of

> *With the power of [air/fire/earth and water], I consecrate this stone*
> *It is now that I make my intention known:*
> *This spirit will be driven away from here,*
> *And then, my environment will be clear.*

7. As the candle and incense burn down— which you should allow them to do

completely—hold the crystal in your dominant hand and meditate upon it. Keep your visualization of your intent strong, and feel the energy of the spirit and its connection to you and your space pouring into the obsidian.

8. Once the candle and incense are completely burned, take the spell's ingredients, along with the crystal, to an open space away from your home. Dispose of all the ingredients except the stone, preferably by burying them in the earth.

9. Hold the stone in your dominant hand and say

> *Spirit, you are trapped, and my [gods/ancestors/guides] have been called upon,*
> *By our will, you will be gone!*

10. Throw the stone as far away from you as possible. Turn around, walk away, and don't look back. The spirit will trouble you no more.

11. Once you have returned home, thoroughly cleanse the house and yourself and re-establish your wards.

CONCLUSION

The only thing you need to get started down the path of magic is yourself. Your power is hidden within, waiting to be tapped into. – Ambrosia Hawthorne

Your power is much more incredible than you probably think. If there is one thing I'd like you to take away from the book, it is this: Within you, you have all the capabilities to protect yourself from psychic or magickal attack. Deep inside, there is a witch within you. All you have to do to be one is make that choice and set yourself on the road less traveled.

This book has been a comprehensive guide for protection magick, covering proactive protection, shielding, hex-breaking, reversal magick, and banishing. Knowing about all of these various spell types before you start your journey will put

you in good stead to go forward and cast magick. Setting up wards is excellent practice and will acclimatize you to magick so that you can then go on to other spell types, such as those for prosperity or finding love.

However, if you are already an accomplished witch, this book has been an addition to your pre-existing library of magickal tomes. It will have supplemented your knowledge of protection magick as well as given you prompts to delve deeper into your practice by considering your own ethical framework as well as ways to adapt spells for your own purposes and even design your own.

If this book has whetted your whistle, you may enjoy my other books on various magickal subjects. I would strongly advise that you never read just one book on magick and think the job is done. The path of the witch is full of spell casting, yes, but to be able to do that, you need to build your knowledge of the field.

I'll end with one final piece of advice: Go forth, delve deeper into magick, and practice, practice, practice. You will achieve things you never thought possible.

Remain magickal, my friends.

REFERENCES

THE BOOK OF SPELLS FOR BEGINNERS

About us. (n.d.). The Satanic Temple. https://thesatanictemple.com/pages/about-us

Ár nDraíocht Féin – our own druidry. (2022). Ár nDraíocht Féin. https://staging.ng.adf.org/

Beyer, C. (2018a, May 2). *An introduction to the basic beliefs of the vodou (voodoo) religion.* Learn Religions. https://www.learnreligions.com/vodou-an-introduction-for-beginners-95712

Beyer, C. (2018b, August 13). *What is chaos magic?* Learn Religions. https://www.learnreligions.com/chaos-magic-95940

Beyer, C. (2019a, January 26). *LaVeyan satanism and the church of satan.* Learn Religions. https://www.learnreligions.com/laveyan-satanism-church-of-satan-95697

Beyer, C. (2019b, January 27). *Understanding the religion of thelema.* Learn Religions. https://www.learnreligions.com/thelema-95700

Chaos magick. (2022, August 2). Encyclopedia.com. https://www.encyclopedia.com/science/encyclopedias-almanacs-transcripts-and-maps/chaos-magick

Connolly, S.B. (2016, June 11). *Bamberg, Germany: The early modern witch burning stronghold.* History... The Interesting Bits! https://historytheinterestingbits.com/2016/06/11/bamberg-germany-the-early-modern-witch-burning-stronghold/

Crowley, A. (1929). *Introduction to magick.* Weiser Books. Thelema 101. https://www.thelema101.com/magick-i

Dugan, P.J. (n.d.). *The origin and practition of pow-wow.* Berks History Center. https://www.berkshistory.org/multimedia/articles/

pow-wow/

Enzheng, T. (2002, January 1). Magicians, magic, and shamanism in ancient China. *Journal of East Asian Archaeology,* *4*(1), 27–73. https://doi.org/10.1163/156852302322454495

Forest, D. (2020, November 30). *Wild magic: Simple ways to step into celtic folk magick.* Llewellyn Worldwide. https://www.llewellyn.com/journal/article/2858

Gardner, Gerald Brousseau. (n.d.). World Religions Reference Library; Encyclopedia.com. https://www.encyclopedia.com/religion/encyclopedias-almanacs-transcripts-and-maps/gardner-gerald-brousseau

Geeraert, A. (2020, August 3). *Kotodama: The spiritual power of words in Japanese culture.* Kokoro Media. https://kokoro-jp.com/culture/1147/

Goêteia explorations in chthonic sorcery. (n.d.). Theomagica. https://theomagica.com/goeteia

Hayward, L. (2020, March 11). *Magic in ancient Greece and rome.* TheCollector. https://www.thecollector.com/magic-in-ancient-greece-and-rome/

Healing and medicine: Healing and medicine in the ancient near east. (2022, June 22). Encyclopedia.com. https://www.encyclopedia.com/environment/encyclopedias-almanacs-transcripts-and-maps/healing-and-medicine-healing-and-medicine-ancient-near-east

History.com Editors. (2017, September 12). *History of witches.* History; A&E Television Networks. https://www.history.com/topics/folklore/history-of-witches

History.com Editors. (2018a, April 6). *Samhain.* History; A&E Television Networks. https://www.history.com/topics/holidays/samhain

History.com Editors. (2018b, March 23). *Wicca.* History;

A&E Television Networks. https://www.history.com/topics/religion/wicca

History.com Editors. (2019, September 27). *Satanism.* History; A&E Television Networks. https://www.history.com/topics/1960s/satanism#anton-lavey

Hosokawa, N. (2014, May 24). *Kotodama: The multifaced Japanese myth of the spirit of language.* OUPblog. https://blog.oup.com/2014/05/kotodama-japanese-spirit-of-language/

Kriebel, D.W. (2002). *Powwowing: A persistent american esoteric tradition.* Esoterica. http://esoteric.msu.edu/VolumeIV/Powwow.htm

Lewis, I.M., & Russell, J.B. (n.d.). *Witchcraft.* Encyclopædia Britannica. https://www.britannica.com/topic/witchcraft

Maccrossan, T. (2002, May 29). *Celtic magic.* Llewellyn Worldwide. https://www.llewellyn.com/encyclopedia/article/193

McAlister, E.A. (n.d.). *Vodou.* Encyclopædia Britannica. https://www.britannica.com/topic/Vodou

Mirelman, S. (2018, August 21). Mesopotamian magic in text and performance. *Mesopotamian Medicine and Magic,* 14, 343–378. https://doi.org/10.1163/9789004368088_018

Naef-Tahvanainen, K. (2014, August 5). *Popular religious practices in China: Shamanism or "wuism."* Life in China Today. https://lifeinchinatoday.com/tag/wuism/

Obeah and myal. (n.d.). Vcu.edu. http://www.people.vcu.edu/~wchan/poco/624/harris_south/Obeah%20and%20Myal.htm

Our courses and membership. (n.d.). Order of Bards, Ovates & Druids. https://druidry.org/our-courses

Pinch, G. (2011, February 17). *Ancient egyptian magic.* Www.bbc.co.uk.

https://www.bbc.co.uk/history/ancient/egyptians/magic_01.shtml

Purkiss, D. (n.d.). *A journey into witchcraft beliefs.* English Heritage. https://www.english-heritage.org.uk/learn/histories/journey-into-witchcraft-beliefs/

Runic magic. (n.d.). National Museum of Denmark. https://en.natmus.dk/historical-knowledge/denmark/prehistoric-period-until-1050-ad/the-viking-age/religion-magic-death-and-rituals/runic-magic/

Said, M. (2018, December). *Mesopotamian magic in the first millennium b.c.* Metmuseum.org; The Metropolitan Museum of Art. https://www.metmuseum.org/toah/hd/magic/hd_magic.htm

Schwemer, D. (2014a, September). *Witchcraft in ancient mesopotamia.* American Society of Overseas Research (ASOR). https://www.asor.org/anetoday/2014/09/witchcraft-in-ancient-mesopotamia/

Schwemer, D. (2014b). *Mesopotamian magic.* Universität Würzburg. https://www.phil.uni-wuerzburg.de/cmawro/magic-witchcraft/mesopotamian-magic/

Storesund, E. (2017, May 1). *Sex, drugs, and drop-spindles: What is seiðr? (Norse metaphysics pt. 2).* Brute Norse. https://www.brutenorse.com/blog/2017/05/sex-drugs-and-drop-spindles-what-is.html

The Editors of Encyclopaedia Britannica. (2021, November 27). *Aleister Crowley.* Encyclopædia Britannica. https://www.britannica.com/biography/Aleister-Crowley

Timon, C.E. (2016, July 22). What is magic to the LaVeyan-satanist ideal type?: A content-analysis of the satanic bible's descriptions of magic.

Anthropology Summer Fellows, *1.* https://digitalcommons.ursinus.edu/cgi/viewconten t.cgi?article=1000&context=anth_sum

Vamvoukakis, A. (n.d.). *Runic magic – history and practice.* The Embroidered Forest. https://theembroideredforest.com/blogs/magic/run ic-magic

Vodou and obeah. (2022, August 26). Gale Library of Daily Life: Slavery in America; Encyclopedia.com. https://www.encyclopedia.com/humanities/applied -and-social-sciences-magazines/vodou-and-obeah

White, M.H. (2020, December 14). Rethinking Aleister Crowley and thelema. *Aries, 21*(1), 1–11. https://doi.org/10.1163/15700593-02101004

Wigington, P. (2019a, May 13). *Biography of Gerald Gardner and the gardnerian wiccan tradition.* Learn Religions. https://www.learnreligions.com/what-is-gardnerian-wicca-2562910

Wigington, p. (2019b, december 28). *Folk magic powwow: history and practices.* Learn religions. Https://www.learnreligions.com/powwow-folk-magic-4779937

CURSE BE GONE

Alejandrez-Prasad, J. (2023, May 22). *Latina Bruja's guide to an egg cleanse (Huevo Limpia).* Pop Sugar. https://www.popsugar.com/smart-living/how-to-do-egg-cleanse-huevo-limpia-ritual-48963277

Alexander, S. (2014). *The modern guide to witchcraft: Your complete guide to witches, covens, & spells.* Adams Media. Amazon Kindle store.

"Am I cursed?" 10 symptoms of magickal danger. (n.d.). Old World Witchcraft. https://oldworldwitchcraft.com/pages/am-i-cursed-10-symptoms-of-magickal-danger

Angel, G. (2013, January 7). *Fascinus & the winged phallus tattoo.* UCL. https://blogs.ucl.ac.uk/researchers-in-museums/2013/01/07/fascinus-the-winged-phallus-tattoo/

Aphrodite titles. (n.d). Theoi Project. https://www.theoi.com/Cult/AphroditeTitles.html

Auryn, M. (2020a). *Psychic witch: A metaphysical guide to meditation, magick & manifestation.* Llewellyn Publications.

Auryn, M. (2020b, January 4). *The difference between charms, amulets & talismans.* Modern Witch. https://www.patheos.com/blogs/modernwitch/2020/01/the-difference-between-charms-amulets-talismans/

Baker, J. (2014). *The cunning man's handbook: The practice of English folk magic 1550–1900.* Avalonia.

Benedetti, A. (2022, October 28). 40 empowering witch quotes that will make you feel wicked. *She Explores Life.* https://sheexploreslife.com/quotes-about-witches/

Beyer, C. (2019, June 5). The five element symbols of fire, water, air, earth, spirit. *Learn Religions.* https://www.learnreligions.com/elemental-symbols-4122788

Blakemore, E. (2016, August 22). A guide to ancient magic. *Smithsonian Magazine.* https://www.smithsonianmag.com/smart-news/guide-ancient-magic-180960129/

Burkert, W. (1987). *Greek religion: Archaic and classical* (J. Raffan, Trans.) Wiley-Blackwell. (Original work published 1977).

Brethauer, A. (2023, May 17). Egg cleanse meaning and powerful ritual interpretation. *The Peculiar*

Brunette.
https://www.thepeculiarbrunette.com/egg-cleanse-meaning-ritual-interpretation/

Chamberlain, L. (2017a, June 6). Magical properties of colors. *Wicca Living.* https://wiccaliving.com/magical-properties-colors/

Chamberlain, L. (2017b, June 16). Clearing and charging ritual tools and magical ingredients. *Wicca Living.* https://wiccaliving.com/clearing-charging-ritual-tools/

Clark, B. (n.d.). Agathos Daimon. *Hellenion.* https://www.hellenion.org/festivals/agathos-daimon/

Cunningham, S. (1989). *Wicca: A guide for the solitary practitioner.* Llewellyn Publications US

Cunningham, S. (2007). *Cunningham's encylopedia of magical herbs.* Llewellyn.

Cunningham, S. (2021). *Cunningham's encylopedia of crystal, gem & metal magic.* Llewellyn.

Curses, hexes, and jinxes: What's the difference? (2020, October 23). Tea and Rosemary. https://teaandrosemary.com/curses-hexes-and-jinxes-whats-the-difference/

Dieleman, J. (2015). The materiality of textual amulets in Ancient Egypt. In: D. Boschung and J. N. Bremmer (Eds.), *The materiality of magic* (pp. 23–58). Wilhelm Fink.

Fowler, R. L. (1995). *Greek magic, Greek religion.* Illinois Classical Studies. https://www.jstor.org/stable/23065394

Golding, W. R. J. (2013). Perceptions of the serpent in the Ancient Near East: Its Bronze Age role in apotropaic magic, healing and protection (Identifier: http://hdl.handle.net/10500/13353) [Masters Dissertation, University of South Africa]. UNISA Institutional Repository.

Habib, R. R. (2017). *Protective magic in Ancient*

Greece: Patterns in the material culture of apotropaia from the archaic to Hellenistic Periods (Publication number FSU_SUMMER2017_Habib_fsu_0071E_13857) [Doctoral Dissertation, Florida State University]. DigiNole.

Harding, J. (2016, June 6). *Sheela Na Gig*. Encylcopedia Britannica. https://www.britannica.com/art/Sheela-Na-Gig

Hargitai, Q. (2018, February 19). *The strange power of the 'evil eye'.* BBC Culture. https://www.bbc.com/culture/article/20180216 -the-strange-power-of-the-evil-eye

Hart, A. (2023, August 19). *Why ancestral curses are so hard to break and how to do it.* The Traveling Witch. https://thetravelingwitch.com/blog/why-generational-curses-are-so-hard-to-break-and-how-to-do-it

Horne, R. (2019). *Folk witchcraft: A guide to lore, land, and the familiar spirit for the solitary practitioner.* Moon over the Mountain Press.

Kelley, G. (2020). Doctor Beaky, the Four Thieves, and De Fabulis Pestis. Contemporary Legend. https://scholarworks.iu.edu/journals/index.php /cl/article/view/35143

Kharis (Χάρις); our relationship with the gods. (2012, July 26). Baring the Aegis. http://baringtheaegis.blogspot.com/2012/07/kh aris-our-relationship-with-gods.html

King, G. (2016). *The British book of spells & charms.* Troy Books.

Konstantinos. (2002). *Vampires: The occult truth.* Llewellyn. Amazon Kindle store.

Kraig, D. M. (2010). *Magic vs. magick.* Llewellyn. https://www.llewellyn.com/blog/2010/05/magi c-vs-magick/

Gottlieb, K. (2017). *Cultural appropriation in contemporary neopaganism and witchcraft.*

(Publication number 304) [Honours dissertation, The University of Maine]. Digital Commons@U Maine. https://digitalcommons.library.umaine.edu/cgi/viewcontent.cgi?article=1303&context=honors

Larson, E. (2019, April 11–13). *Transitional magic: Apotropaic wands as an allegory for the Middle Kingdom* [Conference presentation]. Proceedings of the National Conference On Undergraduate Research (NCUR), Kennesaw State University Kennesaw, Georgia.

Lóránt, V. (2016). Fascinum in Aquicum — protection against evil eye. Phallic amulets in a Roman City. In: H. Erzsébet (Eds.), *Budapest Régiségei* (pp. 63–76). Budapesti Történeti Múzeum.

Meier, A. C. (2019, May 13). *Is there a witch bottle in your house?* Jstor Daily. https://daily.jstor.org/is-there-a-witch-bottle-in-your-house/

Merriam-Webster. (n.d.-a). Occult. *Merriam-Webster.* https://www.merriam-webster.com/dictionary/occult

Merriam-Webster. (n.d.-b). Sigil. *Merriam-Webster.* https://www.merriam-webster.com/dictionary/sigil

Merriam-Webster. (n.d.-c). Ward. *Merriam-Webster.* https://www.merriam-webster.com/dictionary/ward

Montemayor, C. (2023, September 12). *What percentage of men cheat?.* Brides. https://www.brides.com/what-percentage-of-men-cheat-5114527

Moral Relativism. (2022). Ethics Unwrapped. https://ethicsunwrapped.utexas.edu/glossary/moral-relativism

Morningbird. (2023, June 12). *What is a taglock & how it's used in magick.* Magickal Spot. https://magickalspot.com/taglock/

Murphy, J. M. (1990). *Black religion and 'black magic': Prejudice and projection in images of African-derived religions*. Religion, 20(4), 323–339. https://doi.org/10.1016/0048-721X(90)90115-M

Murphy, K. and Susulla, C. (2016). *Secrets of ancient magic: The power of spells, curses, & omens*. Expedition Magazine. https://www.penn.museum/sites/expedition/secrets-of-ancient-magic/

Newman, C. L. (2023). "Savages and sable subjects": White fear, racism, and demonization of New Orleans voodoo in the nineteenth century. Madison Historcal Review, 20(6). https://commons.lib.jmu.edu/mhr/vol20/iss1/6

Offerings to gods and ancestors: Paganism basics. (2018, June 6). Otherworldly Oracle. https://otherworldlyoracle.com/basics-pagan-offerings-to-gods-ancestors/

Olivelle, P. (2023, May 18). Karma. *Encyclopedia Britannica*. https://www.britannica.com/topic/karma

1196 — dried cat. (2021). Museum of Magic and Witchcraft. https://museumofwitchcraftandmagic.co.uk/object/dried-cat/

Parlett, D. (1999). *Tarot*. Encylopedia Britannica. https://www.britannica.com/topic/tarot

Pennick, N. (2021). *The ancestral power of amulets, talismans and mascots: Folk magic in witchcraft & religion*. Destiny Books.

Pinch, G. (2011, February 17). *Ancient Egyptian magic*. BBC History. https://www.bbc.co.uk/history/ancient/egyptians/magic_01.shtml

Porter, G. (2021). *Prayers and protection magick to destroy witchcraft: Banish curses, negative energy & psychic attacks; break spells, evil soul* ties & covenants; protect & release favors. Amazon Kindle store.

Protection Quotes. (n.d.) Bookroo. https://bookroo.com/quotes/protection

Purification in Hellenismos. (2013, July 8). Baring the Aegis. http://baringtheaegis.blogspot.com/2013/07/p urification-in-hellenismos.html

Raine, A. (2012). *The gray witch's grimoire.* John Hunt Publishing. Amazon Kindle store.

The Rider Waite Smith deck. (n.d.). Tarot Heritage. https://tarot-heritage.com/history-4/the-rider-waite-smith-deck/

Saint Thomas, S. (2018, September 25). *Color magic: A witch's guide to color meanings and energies.* Allure. https://www.allure.com/story/color-magic-witchcraft-meanings-guide

Saint Thomas, S. (2020, March 24). *Your guide to the zodiac signs and their elements: Fire, earth, air, and water.* Allure. https://www.learnreligions.com/four-classical-elements-2562825

Schwarcz, J. (2022, February 4). *The evil eye.* McGill Office for Science and Society. https://www.mcgill.ca/oss/article/pseudoscienc e/evil-eye

Sebastiani, A. (2018, July 4). *20 simple yet effective cleansing & purification techniques.* Lady Althaea. https://www.ladyalthaea.com/every-day-is-magickal/cleansing-purification-pt-4

Smith, E. W. (2022, July 11). *These 47 witch quotes are actually magic.* Cosmopolitan. https://www.cosmopolitan.com/lifestyle/a3530 2526/best-witch-quotes/

13 best witch quotes to get you into the October spirit. (2020). The Wholesome Witch. https://www.thewholesomewitch.com/best-witch-quotes/

Thorne, T. (2020). *Protection spells of a wicked witch*. Hentopan Publishing. Amazon Kindle store.

Top 30 quotes on self defense. (n.d.). Girls Who Fight. https://www.girlswhofight.co/post/top-30-quotes-on-self-defense

Uncrossing: Removing negative energy. (2021). Kate's Magik. https://www.katesmagik.com/blogs/news/uncrossing

Versnel, H. S. (1991). *Beyond cursing: The appeal to justice in judicial prayers*. In C. A. Faraone and D. Obbink (Eds.), *Magika hiera: Ancient Greek magic & religion* (pp. 60–106). Oxford University Press.

Vink, F. (2016). *The principles of apotropaic magic on Middle Kingdom wands*. Ancient Egypt.

Virginia. (2019, February 1). *Ancient Greek votive offerings in antiquity: Gifts to the gods*. Ancient & Oriental. *Antiquities*. https://www.antiquities.co.uk/blog/divinity-religion/ancient-greek-votive-offerings-in-antiquity-gifts-to-the-gods/

Visconti, S. (2019). *The complete tarot: Learn the tarot for beginners & advanced (2-in-1 bundle)*. Self-published. Amazon Kindle store.

Volandes, S. (2020, May 14). *The history of the evil eye, an ancient symbol of protection*. Town & Country. https://www.townandcountrymag.com/style/jewelry-and-watches/a32446159/evil-eye-jewelry-history/

Webster, R. (2004, April 19). *Amulets, talismans, & charms*. Llewellyn. https://www.llewellyn.com/journal/article/583

What is a psychic attack? (2022, November 11). College of Psychic Studies. https://www.collegeofpsychicstudies.co.uk/enli

ghten/what-is-a-psychic-attack/

What is magic? Aleister Crowley explains. (2020). Faena Aleph. https://www.faena.com/aleph/what-is-magic-aleister-crowley-explains

Wigington, P. (2017, March 17). *Evoke & invoke.* Learn Religions. https://www.learnreligions.com/evoke-and-invoke-2561892

Wigington, P. (2018a, January 5). *Color magic—magical color correspondences.* Learn Religions. https://www.learnreligions.com/color-magic-magical-correspondences-4105405

Wigington, P. (2018b, March 14). *How to cast a circle for a pagan ritual.* Learn Religions. https://www.learnreligions.com/how-to-cast-a-circle-2562859

Wigington, P. (2018c, December 23). *The Wiccan Rede.* Learn Religions. https://www.learnreligions.com/the-wiccan-rede-2562601

Wiginton, P. (2019a, March 31). *Pagan offerings to the gods.* Learn Religions. https://www.learnreligions.com/offerings-to-the-gods-2561949

Wigington, P. (2019b, May 6). *The four classical elements.* Learn Religions. https://www.learnreligions.com/four-classical-elements-2562825

Wigington, P. (2020, September 21). *9 things to keep on your ancestor altar.* Llewellyn. https://www.llewellyn.com/journal/article/2843

Wilson, D. R (2019, April 26). *Are essential oils safe? 13 things to know before use.* Health Line. https://www.healthline.com/health/are-essential-oils-safe

Witchcraft: Eight myths and misconceptions. (n.d.).

English Heritage. https://www.english-heritage.org.uk/learn/histories/eight-witchcraft-myths/

Woodfield, K. (2022). *Sigil magick: 5 steps to create sigils to manifest your goals*. Self-published. Amazon Kindle store.

SUBSCRIBE TO
SOFIA VISCONTI

Greetings!

As a subscriber, you will receive a **Free Gift** + you will be the first to hear about new books, articles and more exclusives **just for you.**

Simply scan the qr code to join.

SPELLS FOR BEGINNERS, REVERSAL & PROTECTION MAGICK

We sincerely hope you enjoyed our new book **"Spells for Beginners, Reversal & Protection Magick"**. We would greatly appreciate your feedback with an honest review at the place of purchase.

First and foremost, we are always looking to grow and improve as a team. It is reassuring to hear what works, as well as receive constructive feedback on what should improve. Second, starting out as an unknown author is exceedingly difficult, and Amazon reviews go a long way toward making the journey out of anonymity possible. Please take a few minutes to write an honest review.

Best regards,

Sofia Visconti